How to Host a Game Night

How to Host a Game Night

WHAT TO SERVE, WHO TO INVITE, HOW TO PLAY—STRATEGIES *for the* **PERFECT GAME NIGHT**

ERIK ARNESON

TILLER PRESS

NEW YORK   LONDON   TORONTO   SYDNEY   NEW DELHI

An Imprint of Simon & Schuster, Inc.
1230 Avenue of the Americas
New York, NY 10020

Some names and identifying characteristics have been changed.

First Tiller Press trade paperback edition October 2020

TILLER PRESS and colophon are trademarks of Simon & Schuster, Inc.

For information about special discounts for bulk purchases, please contact Simon & Schuster Special Sales at 1-866-506-1949 or business@simonandschuster.com.

The Simon & Schuster Speakers Bureau can bring authors to your live event. For more information or to book an event, contact the Simon & Schuster Speakers Bureau at 1-866-248-3049 or visit our website at www.simonspeakers.com.

Interior design by Jennifer Chung

Manufactured in the United States of America

1 3 5 7 9 10 8 6 4 2

Library of Congress Cataloging-in-Publication Data has been applied for.

ISBN 978-1-9821-5047-1
ISBN 978-1-9821-5048-8 (ebook)

For James Miller

*Thank you for welcoming us
into your wonderful world.*

^^^^^^^^^^^^^^

Contents

Author's Note

While I was writing this book, a lot of wonderful people told me a lot of fascinating stories, many of which are recounted here. I generally use people's real names, but in some cases pseudonyms are used at the request of those who shared with me.

Introduction: A Great Time to Be a Gamer

These days the bulk of our entertainment exists on screens. Between phones, tablets, computers, and televisions, the average American spends more than eleven hours a day on their devices, according to a 2018 report from the marketing research company Nielsen. Even books, magazines, and newspapers are often read on electronic devices.

So why is it that board games and card games are, by almost any measure, better and more popular than ever?

There are some analog reasons, such as spending time with friends and family and improving cognitive function. In one study, the risk of dementia was 15 percent lower among those who played board games than in those who did not;[1] in another, playing board games was associated with higher cognitive function at age seventy;[2] in a third study, playing the ancient game of Go for two hours a day five days a week led to "significant improvements" among children with ADHD.[3] And don't underestimate the appeal of plain old nostalgia. There's something timeless and wonderful about gathering around a game table, even if many of your gaming memories involve family squabbles while playing Monopoly on Thanksgiving.

But ironically, much of the credit for the current renaissance of tabletop gaming must be given to those very same digital devices we're so obsessed with. The thing is, you can only buy what you can find, and what takes a few seconds today (thanks to those devices) used to take a lot of effort.

Before the internet, most people bought games at big-box stores like Toys"R"Us and Walmart. By the very nature of those stores, the games that appeared there were expected to sell hundreds of thousands if not millions of copies, making it rare to see a game without a familiar publisher such as Milton Bradley (acquired by Hasbro in 1984), Parker Brothers (acquired by Hasbro in 1991), Selchow and Righter (the original North American publisher of Scrabble and Trivial Pursuit, aquired by Hasbro via Coleco in 1989), Mattel, Ideal, and Pressman. Local toy shops tended to have a limited selection of tabletop games, and those they did carry were usually children's games. There were dedicated game stores here and there, along with a few mail-order opportunities—the Baltimore-based game company Avalon Hill, for example, included an order form for additional games in its game boxes—but finding quality new games that could be enjoyed by adults was generally accomplished by only a dedicated few.

Today, it's an entirely different story. Thousands of new games are published every year, many by small, creative companies that simply would never have been able to survive without the ability to connect with customers via the internet.

At Kickstarter, the most popular crowdfunding website, the games category has generated more revenue than any other, and tabletop games—including board games, card games, and roleplaying games— are the biggest success stories by far. Project backers pledged more than $176 million to more than 2,700 successful tabletop game projects in 2019, vastly outpacing the $16 million pledged to video games.[4] And Kickstarter's impact on the board game industry continues to grow: On May 1, 2020, the epic fantasy board game Frosthaven became the most successful board game ever launched on the service, raising nearly $13 million from more than 83,000 backers.[5] Not every game launched on Kickstarter is funded, but those numbers are solid evidence that the world of indie game design and publishing has never been stronger.

That's great for gamers because it means we're treated to an ever-increasing number of fantastic games.

Impressive as that $176 million is, it's still a small slice of the overall tabletop gaming pie. For example, Hasbro, whose game catalog includes evergreen titles like Monopoly, Magic: The Gathering, and Dungeons & Dragons, reported more than $1.5 billion in revenue from its gaming category in 2019,[6] up more than 21 percent over the past five years.[7]

Just as the internet has made it easier to find exciting new games, it has also made it simple for gamers to find one another and share their thoughts about those games. One of the best resources is the website BoardGameGeek.com, which boasts an amazing database of games rated by gamers around the world and is home to a dazzling variety of videos, game reviews and previews, game designer diaries, forums, and much more. The Geek, as it's affectionately known, has a huge influence on the hobby gaming industry, best explained by a few numbers: BGG has 2.5 million registered users (I'm proud to be number 48), 5 million unique visitors every month, and nearly 100 million page views per month. Game publishers love seeing their games appear on The Hotness, the Geek's constantly updated list of the fifteen most-viewed game pages that's displayed, by default, on every page of the site. (And BGG users love to debate how much impact being listed on The Hotness really has!)

Scott Alden cofounded BGG in 2000 while working full-time as a video game software developer. Six years later, the website had become so popular that he left his other job to run the company, one of the earliest signs of the dramatic expansion the board game industry was about to undergo. The Geek now has twenty employees and seventy-five volunteer administrators. In addition to running the multifaceted website, BGG hosts two BGG.con game conventions in the Dallas area every year, plus one on a cruise ship.

Another early sign of the pending board game renaissance was the

2005 emergence of *The Dice Tower*, a podcast created by Tom Vasel. Over the past fifteen years *The Dice Tower* has grown into an entity that hosts more than two dozen podcasts (including three of my favorites: *This Game Is Broken*, *Ludology*, and *Board Games Insider*), organizes annual conventions (one on each coast of the U.S. and a third on a cruise ship), presents an annual set of board game awards, and creates far too many videos to count: *The Dice Tower* YouTube channel typically posts six new videos every day. Six new videos. Every. Day. Six! It's fair to call *The Dice Tower* a small media empire.

Speaking of YouTube, Wil Wheaton's *Tabletop* premiered there in 2012 and ran through 2017. On that show, Wheaton and some of his celebrity friends played games like Dead of Winter, Lords of Vegas, and Love Letter. More than 3.6 million people have watched Wheaton and his friends play The Resistance. In 2013, the show helped launch International Tabletop Day, which became a worldwide celebration of tabletop games. The popularity of *Tabletop*, its successor show (in spirit if not in actuality) *Game the Game*, and other board game–focused YouTube channels such as Shut Up & Sit Down (274,000 subscribers), Watch It Played (188,000), BoardGameGeek's main channel (112,000), and Man vs Meeple (57,000) is a true measure of how dramatically the tabletop games industry has grown. Twenty-five years ago, very few people around the world made a living designing board games; today, people make a living creating YouTube videos *about* board games.

With board games exploding throughout popular culture, the buyers at big-box retailers like Target and Barnes & Noble started to take notice. Board games—and not just the perennial best sellers or games published by huge companies—appeared on their shelves. Seemingly overnight, what could easily have stayed a niche trend became mainstream. Wits & Wagers, a terrific trivia game from indie publisher North Star Games, is a perfect example of this transition. At the time Wits & Wagers first appeared in Target in 2006, North Star Games had two employees, both of whom had gone without a salary for much of the company's three-year existence. Now fourteen years later, the game has sold nearly two million copies and the company has grown significantly. Yet as brilliant as it is, Wits & Wagers may never have been sold in Target if not for the overwhelmingly positive attention it first garnered from websites like BoardGameGeek and About.com, along with the internet's ability to spread the news of the awards it won from places like Mensa, *Games* magazine, and the *Milwaukee Journal Sentinel*.

So, yeah. The impact of the internet on today's amazing board game scene cannot be overstated. But neither can the importance of the explosion in game variety over the last two decades. A visit to your local game shop, or Target, or Amazon, or any online game store will reveal a dizzying array of options. The BoardGameGeek database, by far the best single source of information about published games, shows that thirty-one years ago—in 1989—nearly 900 games and expansions were published. That number grows dramatically in later decades: about 1,200 games in 1999, more than 3,300 games in 2009, and an unbelievable 5,000 games in 2019. That's more than a dozen new games every day.

Quantity alone means nothing. But among those thousands of games have been many bona fide gems, games of remarkable creativity and depth with a previously unthinkable assortment of themes. Wingspan, an award-winning strategy game designed by Elizabeth Hargrave in which players compete to attract the best birds to their network of wildlife preserves, is an international hit and was featured in the *Wall Street Journal*. Pandemic, Matt Leacock's cooperative game where players work to eradicate diseases across the globe, has been a best seller for more than a decade. If you're a fan of zombies, or opera, or football (whatever that word means to you), or pandas, or the fashion industry, there's a game for you.

Truly, there has never been a better time to be a gamer.

And I should know. I've been playing board games since the mid-

1970s, when my younger sister, Lisa, and I faced off with classics like Sorry! and Connect 4 and played Monopoly and Clue with our parents. Diplomacy became a favorite in high school, while Euchre and Risk took center stage at college. By 1999, I had fallen headfirst into the world of German and European games like Settlers of Catan, Elfenland, and Adel Verpflichtet. For about a decade and a half, I wrote about board games for the website formerly known as About.com. (It has since morphed into the media company Dotdash, and some of the articles I wrote are still featured at The Spruce.) My personal game collection topped out at more than a thousand until I undertook a focused effort to get it down to a more reasonable size through 2018 and 2019. Today, I own about three hundred games, most of which are contained in thirty-six square feet of shelves from Ikea. (By the way, if you need game shelves, I highly recommend the Kallax line, but more on that in chapter 5.)

How to Host a Game Night is my love letter to game nights. Whether it's a quiet evening at home with my wife, Beth, a lazy Sunday afternoon with a handful of friends, a holiday spent with family, or a daylong gathering of thirty die-hard gamers, game time is my Zen time. It's a chance to cut loose, to play, to stay connected with old friends and make some new ones. Few things are better than getting a group of friends together on a Thursday night to relax over a beer and a few friendly rounds of Can't Stop and Sagrada.

As fun as game nights are, hosting one—especially for the first time—can be intimidating. There are so many wonderful board games . . . should you choose ahead of time? Let your guests pick? What game will set the right tone and make sure everyone has fun? And the pressure of choosing the right game is just the half of it! What food do you serve? When do you tell guests to arrive? How late will they stay? Where are you going to put everyone?!

Trust me, I get it. Over the years Beth and I have hosted a lot of game nights, game days, and even ten-day-long game events. When we started, we had no idea what we were doing. We spent days preparing the first time we invited a group of friends over to our house, and we were scurrying around, trying to finish things up right until the doorbell rang. Thankfully, we've learned a few things along the way. Decide what games you want to play in advance and learn the rules. Whenever possible, serve drinks in bottles—with lids. And relax, because game night will be fun.

Some relatively simple planning can greatly reduce any stress you're feeling. Whether you want a quiet night of two-player games or a weekend-long event with a dozen friends at a cabin on the shore of Lake Superior; whether you're a first-time host or a seasoned pro looking to level up your gatherings, you'll find plenty of tips and tricks to give you the tools and confidence you need to host an unforgettable night. At the end of most chapters, you'll find a section highlighting some great games to inspire you and get you started off on the right foot.

As you plan your next (or first!) game night, remember that the goal is to have fun, to share smiles with your friends and family, and to create memories that will strengthen your bonds. Do that, and you're in for some good times. Game on!

1

The Ground Rules

When I'm not playing board games, I'm a hobbyist woodworker. Like many woodworkers, one of my heroes is Norm Abram, longtime master carpenter on *This Old House* and former host of *The New Yankee Workshop*. When Abram wrote a book of advice culled from his decades of work, he titled it *Measure Twice, Cut Once.* "Measure twice, cut once" is a cardinal rule in woodworking because mistakes at the measuring stage will lead to exponentially larger problems—and serious headaches—down the road. Preparing adequately at the start of a project helps everything else go smoothly.

The same concept holds true for many things in life, including game nights: most often what makes a game night successful isn't the games you play or the food you eat—it's all the work you, as the host, do in advance. Laying the groundwork for a successful game night doesn't have to be difficult, but it does take a little focused effort to make your guests comfortable and ensure the night goes smoothly.

PREPARING FOR A SUCCESSFUL GAME NIGHT

Before our friends Tom and Dana Diehl moved a few hundred miles away (due to a job change, not to avoid me, or so I've been assured), they hosted semiregular game nights. These were usually six-player gatherings, involving Beth and me along with another couple, Mark and Amy Hager. Tom, Mark, and I were roommates when we attended Temple University, so we have a long history of gaming together. At Temple in the late 1980s and early 1990s, we played countless hands of the traditional trick-taking card game Euchre with an occasional foray into global domination via Risk.

By the time we were getting together at Tom and Dana's house, the entire gaming landscape had changed. Games like Catan, Dixit, and Dominion were (or would soon be) international hits. We helped playtest the original Betrayal at House on the Hill, a game that caused Mark to constantly wonder, "Who on earth is letting children wander into this house?" At one memorable session, we learned how terrible we all are at the dexterity game Ring-O Flamingo, in which players launch life preservers toward flamingos on an elevated board while trying to avoid alligators. If you're ever counting on one of us to toss you a life preserver, I apologize in advance. And please be sure to have your affairs in order.

We loved going to Tom and Dana's for game night. Dana always had a great spread of food and drinks, and Tom . . . well, I'm sure Tom must have done something. The first floor of their house was open concept before *open concept* became the most common phrase uttered on HGTV and we played in the dining area, between the kitchen and the living room, a perfect location with plenty of bright light. It was, above all, a comfortable place to be. Tom and Dana were great hosts because they made us feel welcome. The care and consideration that went into not just the food and drink but also the company we kept, the games we played, and the way they set up the house to make it easy to play all added up to a terrific evening time and time again.

As a host, you're responsible for the experience of your guests. Erin Fiscus, who hosts regular game nights with her husband, Josiah, puts it well: "People have fun when I want people to feel welcome and comfortable the moment they walk in my door." I couldn't agree more, and that process starts with setting clear expectations.

SETTING EXPECTATIONS

Let's be honest, scheduling a game night is easy. There are two steps: (1) Set a place, date, and time. (2) Let people know. *Boom.* Mission accomplished. Let's play games!

Not so fast. While it's true that game nights are generally casual, laid-back events, inviting a bunch of people over is sure to bring questions—many of which your guests may never ask out of a sense of politeness, but which they'll have anyway. Should I bring games? Food? Can I bring a friend? Are we playing silly wacky party games or heavy thinky strategy games? If I show up late, will everyone already be playing a game, leaving me to wander the room awkwardly watching other people have fun? Will Sean be there?

A prepared host will preempt at least a few of those questions in their invitation. Properly setting expectations involves more than answering the basic questions of where and when. Longtime game-night host John R. Ilko is a pro at this. He hosts two monthly game nights at his house, one on the second Friday of the month, the other on the fourth Saturday of the month. His invitations, sent by email to about three dozen friends, go something like this:

Hey, everyone! Tomorrow is the second Friday in January, so let's play some games! I'd love to play Terraforming Mars with the Turmoil expansion, but if you'd like to play anything else specific, please yell it out, and we'll try to have it on hand. If it makes you happy, feel free to bring a soda or what-have-you. It's definitely not necessary, and we'll have snacks on hand. We're going to get started right at 5 p.m., so if you're able to make it, shoot me an email or text so that we can know how many to plan for. See you soon!

This is a great invitation. Friendly and welcoming, full of details, yet short enough that people are likely to read the entire thing. John points out that snacks and simple beverages will be provided, letting guests know that a full meal will not. Especially for an after-work game night, that's crucial information. Many people do prepare full meals and provide beer, wine, or cocktails at their game nights and anything is fair game. Your duty as host is to let people know so they can plan accordingly.

In the same spirit, John's invitation tells you what type of games are going to be on the table. Terraforming Mars is brilliant in many ways, but it's a two-hour (or more) strategy game that boasts a sixteen-page rulebook. It's not for everyone. Then again, no game is. One woman's Gloomhaven is another man's Bananagrams, and that's one of the first things you need to realize before hosting a game night. Not everyone is going to like the same games, and that's okay. I'm flexible when it comes to choosing games; it's easy enough to convince me to dive into a deep strategy title like Terraforming Mars or Twilight Struggle, and I love playing party games like Codenames and Just One. Many people have stronger preferences. No matter what games speak to you, give your guests fair warning so they can show up with bells on or bow out as they see fit.

One final but essential note about John's invitation: he's very clear about the start time for the event. When it comes to game night, guests who show up fashionably late can mean a delayed start to the game or inadvertently leaving people out. We'll talk more about the flow of a game night in chapter 4, but if you need to start at a certain time, be clear with your guests. If you *are* planning to be flexible, you'll still want a sense of when folks plan to arrive, so be sure to ask that they let you know when they RSVP.

BEFORE THE GUESTS ARRIVE

There are a few things every host should do that almost go without saying. Cleaning is one of them, but you'd be surprised by how many people get so wrapped up in choosing the game and setting up the board that they forget to wipe down the bathroom. You want your home to look far more presentable than the apartment Tom, Mark, and I shared in college. (It's amazing we made it out of there alive.) As game-night veteran Vanessa Shannen-Anderson says, "You're hosting, make sure your house is tidy. Some people get uncomfortable with a messy place, especially if there's food near their very expensive games." However, Vanessa adds, it's important to not obsess. "Don't worry about making it perfect," she says. "Everyone is going to have fun."

Clean any room that guests are likely to use, especially the game room and the bathroom. It's also a good idea to have hand sanitizer and wipes available for guests who may be concerned about germs. In many games, the components are passed among players with great regularity, and it can help to clean those pieces periodically. *Con crud* is the slang term for any illness that spreads at a game convention. You don't want the same to happen at your game night!

Food and drink are also high on the list of must-do prep work. The last thing you want is for your guests to walk in ready to play games only to discover you frantically making guacamole. Whether you take a minimalist approach or channel your inner Bobby Flay and cook spice-crusted salmon, you need to decide at least a day or two before game night to give yourself time to shop and prepare.

Experienced game-night host Jeremy Thigpen has a fantastic checklist of sorts to help prep for a game night that goes well beyond cleaning: he makes sure there's ice in the freezer, builds a music playlist on YouTube, sends invitations by text, lets the neighbors know about game night since he lives in a town house, solicits game ideas, and—on those occasions when the session is going to last twelve hours or so—orders a trophy or prize that fits the theme of the games they'll be playing.

While you wait for a text from Jeremy (hit me up, Jeremy!), remember that your game nights should reflect your personality. Some people go all out. Others prefer a more laid-back approach. It's all good. What matters is that you and your guests are comfortable and everyone has a good time.

There are, though, two indispensable pieces of preparation specific to game nights. The first is laying out the games. If you know exactly who's coming over and what you're going to play, having the game completely set up before anyone arrives is ideal. I love showing up to a game night where we can jump right in. Having the table ready to go when your first guests arrive sends a clear message that game night is important to you and you value their time. If you haven't chosen a specific game, no worries. Place a stack of four or five options on the table to help focus the conversation about what to play. When I go to a friend's house and see hundreds of games on their shelves, I could spend an hour happily browsing their collection. If you want to actually play a game, that's a problem! I'll see dozens of games that look great and never settle on one. By narrowing the choices to a handful of preselected options, you're doing me—and your other guests—a favor.

Second, you need to learn the rules to the games you expect to play.

THE ART OF EXPLAINING GAME RULES

If playing a game is the equivalent of eating a big piece of cherry pie (or whatever your own favorite dessert is, although science conclusively proves the correct answer is cherry pie), learning the rules of a game is the equivalent of eating a large helping of broccoli. That is, unless you like broccoli—in which case maybe you like learning game rules, too, and we should become friends so you can teach me all the rules. But we need to eat our vegetables, and teaching game rules well is essential to keeping a game night flowing and fun. Generally, teaching the rules is the responsibility of the person who owns the game. The host, however, should make sure the game owner is ready to go—and if they aren't, the host needs to either find a volunteer or take on the responsibility themselves.

The good news is that teaching the rules is a skill that can be learned. And if I can learn it—at least to the point where I do a serviceable job—trust me, you can learn it, too. Teaching rules is such a substantial and 100 percent unavoidable part of game night, I'm going to spend a fair amount of time discussing it. You're free to skip ahead, of course, but if you do I'm confident you'll be back soon enough—just like what happens when you skip ahead in a rulebook.

My favorite person to learn a new game from is my friend James Miller. He starts each game by announcing in his smooth, radio-quality voice something like, "Welcome to the wonderful world of Pandemic." (And, yes, the only time the words *wonderful world* can be associated with *pandemic* is when James is teaching the rules to a game.)

Teaching the rules well and efficiently is essential because, frankly, most of us don't have much patience for the process. Totally understandable—after all, people are there to play the game!—but playing the game well means knowing the rules, so you need to get creative and keep it short. Rodney Smith, host of the BoardGameGeek YouTube channel Watch It Played, is a master of this. Rodney's natural charisma and easygoing style make it downright fun to learn the rules. And I'm clearly not alone in thinking so. His video explaining the rules of Scythe, a heavy strategy game set in an alternate-history version of the 1920s, has been watched more than nine hundred thousand times. More than sixty of Rodney's videos have been watched at least a hundred thousand times.

So when Rodney offers advice about explaining a game's rules, I listen. And he doesn't hold back when describing how much the success of a game night rests on the shoulders of those who explain the games. "I think the rules teach is the most important aspect of the game night," Rodney says. "The teach will be most people's first experience of the game, and it will either set them off on a journey of adventure they feel well equipped to take on, or it will leave them lost and confused, and in bad spirits."

I wholeheartedly agree. Understanding a game's rules is essential to enjoying the experience. Going into a game confused about how to collect resources or how to score points is a surefire recipe for frustration. As a player, you don't necessarily need to know every nook and cranny of the rulebook the first time you play a game, but you sure want to be confident that someone at the table does. Now, that doesn't mean the teacher is doomed to carry the weight of the world all on their own. If you have a group that's open to this, it's perfectly fine to ask people to watch a short video ahead of time—or, if you're truly nervous about teaching the rules and there's no other option, you can watch it together at game night. Seriously, if you're trying to learn a game and Rodney has a video explaining the rules, save yourself some time and watch his video. I've learned many games that way and often use his videos as a way to judge whether I want to buy a game I've been considering. Another must is checking to see if anyone has uploaded a player aid or rules summary to BoardGameGeek. Many popular games have tremendously helpful user-created player aids and summaries.

When your guests have assembled at the table, Rodney and James both recommend starting with the game's theme to give them an over-all sense of what's going on in the game. After the theme, Rodney says, there should be "a tour of the components, then the objective, and then a general sense of the gameplay." James adds, "Another very important thing to point out early, and often, is how to score. Or how not to lose."

Only then should you get into the real details.

You won't be able to do a good job of any of that if the first time you're opening the rulebook is when everyone is seated at the table. Preparation is key. Let's use Horrified as an example. Horrified is a family strategy game in which everyone works together to defeat various monsters like Dracula and the Creature from the Black Lagoon. Prior to game night, James and Rodney would set aside between thirty and ninety minutes to learn the rules for Horrified well enough that they're comfortable explaining them. It may require less time for a simpler game and more for a complicated one. However long it takes, don't skimp on this step. "Too many hosts don't give themselves enough time," Rodney says. "They're forced to rush, leaving some of the rule learning [until] the gamers are there—which can create a disjointed teaching session." I've learned this lesson the hard way many times. Unless you want irate guests, arguments, or near chaos, it's a terrible idea to be teaching yourself at the same time you're teaching your guests.

James and Rodney both believe in a solo practice session whenever possible, teaching the game to no one in particular but running through their entire presentation to make certain it sounds coherent. "I like to know the rules well enough that I can explain the game without referring to the rulebook," James says. "I want to absorb the rules and understand them so I can put them in my own words." Their approaches to learning a game do differ slightly. Rodney prefers to set up the full game in front of him while he learns; James tends not to.

They both spend time looking through the game's components, such as any tokens, markers, cards, and figures, to be sure they know what function they serve and what they're called. "When I explain the game, however, I do not necessarily stick to the names the rules use, especially if they use obtuse names," James says. "If the names correspond nicely with the theme, perhaps I will use the correct names." In other words, don't use unnecessary jargon. Some groups I've played with refer to the money within a game by the exact term used in the rules—lira in Viticulture, credits in Xia: Legends of a Drift System, or elecktro in Power Grid—and that approach can add to the atmosphere of gameplay and enhance the sense of theme. But many groups enjoy the same games just as much by referring to the money as—generically and admittedly U.S.-centrically—*dollars*. Know your group's preferences and adjust your presentation accordingly.

Another key point: encourage questions! People may hesitate to ask questions for fear of looking stupid. Alleviate their concern by stopping periodically to see if anyone has questions. That doesn't mean you have to answer every question right away. If the question fits better later in the explanation, it's fine to say, "Great question. We'll get to that in a minute."

At the same time, it's critical to not leave out anything significant. "Be thorough, but not to the point of obsession," is how James puts it. In some cases, it makes sense to delay a portion of the rules explanation until the game is underway—but be careful if you do this and tell the other players what you're doing and why. As James says, "No one wants to be halfway through the game and hear, 'Oh yeah, there's this other rule I should have told you.'"

Yep. The infamous midgame "I forgot one thing." I can hear your exasperated sighs from here and all I can say is I've been there. I call these games *asterisk games* and have played dozens, maybe hundreds, of them through the years. Come to think of it, every game I've lost was an asterisk game. . . . Odd. Seriously, having been on both ends of the one-more-thing moment, it's never fun. If you teach a game and leave out one rule, it will inevitably be a rule that—when revealed— undoes the entire strategy of one player who's been working up to a massive, game-changing play for the last forty-five minutes. Probably the grumpiest player. All you can do is apologize, and hope that eve- ryone can move on. If you're on the receiving end of a midgame rule reveal, be kind. The person teaching you the game didn't mean to leave it out. Take a deep breath, ask for any clarity you need, and play on. It is, after all, only a game. (If you suspect the rule was left out intention- ally, politely ask where the restroom is, climb out the window, and go home. That's borderline psychotic behavior, and you should never play another game with someone who does that.)

Now that you've taken in James's and Rodney's expert advice, I recommend watching the YouTube video "How to Teach Board Games Like a Pro," produced by the team at Shut Up & Sit Down. Host Quintin Smith (better known as Quinns) calls explaining the game rules "the worst part of any board game night" but offers simple, concrete sug- gestions to make it better. He boils the process down to ten excellent tips, including: use examples, ask if the players want a dummy round before the real game starts, and do not try a tag team approach to teach- ing game rules. I strongly endorse all of those, especially the last one. Trying to learn a game from two or more people at the same time is typically a miserable experience. Actually, strike *typically* and insert *always*.

One final tip before we leave the broccoli section of this book: if you're in the middle of a game and a rules question comes up that you can't find quickly in the rulebook, google it. Very specifically. For exam- ple, searching "Azul what happens if a player can't fit tiles on a pattern line" will lead you to a discussion on BoardGameGeek where you'll instantly learn that it's bad news for that player. If they can't put any tiles on their pattern line, where tiles score positive points, they still have to pick some up and put them on their floor line, where tiles score negative points. I can't count the number of times I've googled a specific rules question and found it answered on BoardGameGeek or Reddit, often by either the designer or publisher.

TEACHING GAME RULES: DOS AND DON'TS

DO:
- Watch a rules explanation video.
- Practice your presentation.
- Start with the theme and the overall goal.
- Incorporate and explain the game's components.
- Use plenty of examples.
- Encourage questions.

DON'T:
- Read from the rulebook.
- Let other players "help" you explain the rules.
- Forget anything important!

Two-Player Game Nights

They say that the eyes are the window to the soul. But I once heard someone claim that the best way to get to know a person, to see their unvarnished inner self, is to play a board game with them. I believe it, and so does Bonnie Winston, a matchmaker and relationship expert. "Games can show us who we really are," she says. "The true essence of people can come out in a game situation. They say you don't really know a person until you travel or live with them, but I think you should play a board game with them, too!"

Playing games reveals profound truths about how we treat others, how we respond to unexpected situations, how we think about and solve problems, and how we handle both winning and losing. Two-player games, in particular, let you see what the other person is made of. Do they take a hypercompetitive, win-at-all-costs approach, or are they able to relax, smile, and carry on a conversation during the game? If you do something wrong, are they able to point it out with kindness? And how do they respond if you point out a mistake of theirs?

You may not instantly think of a game night as involving only two players. You probably don't need to send an invitation, certainly not a formal one, and you may very well be living with your opponent. One-on-one game nights are a special opportunity to strengthen bonds with someone you care about: a romantic partner, a good friend, a child. Sometimes the quiet intimacy of playing a game with one other person is the perfect game night.

GAME NIGHT AS A MEET-CUTE

We're suckers for the meet-cute trope in romantic comedies because it works so well. A meet-cute is typically a charming first encounter between the two romantic leads in a film. Maybe they bump into each other and one spills a bit of juice on the other, or perhaps one is a comedian heckled by the other during a set. Although game nights don't come with a script—unless you're talking about the movie *Game Night,* which is hilarious to watch but which you definitely don't want to replicate—they can be a great way to strengthen romantic bonds and meet potential partners. A surprising number of people have fallen in love at a game night, or even met the person they wound up spending the rest of their life with.

Couples like Nate Beeler and Lizzy Palmer can testify firsthand to the ability of games to spark a long-term romance. They struck up a conversation at the 2008 Gathering of Friends—an annual eleven-day event organized by Alan R. Moon, designer of games like Ticket to Ride and Elfenland—after admiring each other's T-shirts (he had on a Bob Ross "Happy Little Trees" T-shirt; she was wearing a Domo-kun face tee) and found they had a lot in common. Because they lived on opposite sides of the United States, playing board games online proved to be an excellent way to build their relationship. Through many nights of playing Can't Stop and other games, Nate learned that Lizzy is "incredibly sweet, funny, and patient"; in turn, Lizzy learned that Nate "will do anything, no matter how embarrassing, for a point in party games." Nate and Lizzy have been married for eight years now, and they say they owe not just their marriage but the majority of their friend circle to games and fellow gamers.

Falling in love is never an exact science, but there is plenty of evidence to suggest that board games do prime us to strengthen our romantic bonds. In fact, a 2019 study conducted at Baylor University, "Examining Couple Recreation and Oxytocin Via the Ecology of Family Experiences Framework," showed that when couples play board games together, their bodies release extra oxytocin—sometimes referred to as the "cuddle hormone" or the "love hormone."[1] Previous research on oxytocin—such as Sara B. Algoe, Laura E. Kurtz, and Karen Grewen's 2017 study "Oxytocin and Social Bonds: The Role of Oxytocin in Perceptions of Romantic Partners' Bonding Behavior"—revealed that the hormone appears to help strengthen the bonds between romantic partners, as well as between mothers and infants.[2]

The Baylor study, published in the *Journal of Marriage and Family*, was conducted by Karen Melton, PhD, assistant professor of child and family studies, and Maria Boccia, PhD, professor of child and family studies. Dr. Melton and Dr. Boccia studied twenty couples who were evenly divided between taking a couple's art class and playing board games like backgammon, checkers, and chess. "Our big finding was that all couples release oxytocin when playing together—and that's good news for couples' relationships," Dr. Melton said in a February 12, 2019, press release. Dr. Melton and Camilla Hodge, PhD, assistant professor of health, kinesiology, and recreation at the University of Utah, will continue to research the impact of recreational activities, including board games, on romantic relationships. Although her first study did not specifically look at cooperative games versus competitive games, Dr. Melton says she plans to do so in the future. She's inclined to think that playing cooperative games would have an even stronger effect. "We believe that positive communication, touch, and responsiveness may be the key factors at play for positive connections," she says.

Beyond our physiological response, breaking out the board games can be a great way to learn more about someone. After reading about the Baylor study and trading emails with Dr. Melton, I reached out to Terri Orbuch, PhD, a relationship expert, distinguished professor at Oakland University in Michigan, and author of *5 Simple Steps to Take Your Marriage from Good to Great*. She says that "depending on the type of game that's played, you can learn how your partner responds to competition and stress, how your partner answers specific questions, and how you work together if you're playing on a team. In a team game, you can see if your partner is encouraging, or if they get upset when they don't win or you don't know an answer. Do you work well together, or does your partner take charge and not focus on your strengths?"

Tery and Mark Noseworthy certainly learned a lot about each other by gaming together. Tery was introduced to Mark at a Gathering of Friends event, but it wasn't until a mutual friend who hosted weekly game nights close to her home invited them both to attend that they truly started to get to know each other. She and Mark began dating in January 2000, about nine months after they first met. Tery says playing games "gave us a good view into each other's strengths and weaknesses, as well as sense of humor and personality. We each got to see each other interacting with both new people and people we had known awhile, and we got to see how we react in confusing and difficult situations, too." They got married in 2005.

Games that ask personal questions and pose dilemmas—like Say Anything, 5 Second Rule, and Loaded Questions (or its cousin, Where's the Money, Lebowski?)—can also be revealing since you may learn things you wouldn't otherwise know about your partner's opinions and beliefs. As Dr. Orbuch points out, "One trait of happy couples is that they continue to get to know each other—their inner lives and social worlds, what makes them tick. Over time, partners stop asking the questions they used to ask when they were first dating. You may be surprised to learn a thing or two by simply asking questions you never thought to ask. This will create intimacy, add surprise, and increase passion and excitement in a relationship."

Dr. Orbuch says that while people "often think of relationships in terms of support, security, and family, relationships are also about fun, laughter, and personal growth. Given the challenges and stress in today's world, playing games reminds couples of the importance of having fun with your partner." Games, she adds, can reignite the passion in a relationship.

Not every meet-cute romance in the movies turns out like you'd hope or expect, and that's true in real life as well. "I had a girlfriend in college I met playing Dungeons & Dragons," says Frank Branham, cohost of *The Ascent of Board Games* podcast. "It went from D&D to drunken D&D to dating and then living together for a couple of years. Then she married our Dungeon Master."

THE JOY OF COOPERATIVE GAMES

An old adage holds that there are three kinds of people in the world: those who can count, and those who cannot. I'm pretty sure something's wrong with that saying but I've never put my finger on exactly what. At any rate, tabletop games can be divided into three kinds: competitive, semi-cooperative, and cooperative.

Competitive games are by far the most common type of tabletop game, and most people are used to the notion that only one player will win. Many of us have seen firsthand that certain types of competitive games can bring out strong emotions. Games in which players directly attack one another can—with the wrong players—lead to real-world conflict. Risk is a classic example, but any game involving territory or combat seems to spark a heightened competitive intensity. On occasion, competitive games provide an unintended opportunity for simmering issues unrelated to the game itself to bubble over, as with family members who may be dealing with a stressful home life.

Semi-cooperative games, in which most players are united but may not know who among them is working against the group's interest, play best with more than two players (often many more than two players), so we'll discuss them in detail in chapter 4.

Which brings us to cooperative games, one of my favorite genres. As much fun as it is to win on my own, something about being part of a team makes victory a notch or two sweeter. The greatest gaming experience of my life was when a group of friends and I completed Pandemic Legacy: Season 1—a game that takes at least twelve hours, and more likely twenty or so, to finish the entire campaign—over the course of a single weekend. Pandemic Legacy and its precursor, Pandemic, are perhaps the best-known of the cooperative genre of board games. Designer Matt Leacock created the original Pandemic in part because competitive games weren't working for him and his wife, Donna. "I recall a particularly disastrous negotiation game where the emotions generated by my psychological manipulation, relentless competition, and betrayals during play bled out into the real world and put a strain on our relationship," Leacock wrote in a March 2020 op-ed for *The New York Times*.

In cooperative games, players compete against the game itself rather than against one another. In Pandemic, published in 2008, members of an elite disease control team race against the clock to cure four diseases that are spreading across the world in sometimes unpredictable ways. Each player has a unique role with a special ability to help the team; the scientist, for example, is better at finding cures, while the dispatcher can move people vast distances. But the challenges are many. Every turn, new disease cubes are added to the board and you're never far from an outbreak. Winning Pandemic requires cooperation, skill, and a little luck.

Reiner Knizia's Lord of the Rings, published in 2000, wasn't the first cooperative board game, but it was the first to earn widespread acclaim among hobbyist gamers. It helped inspire Leacock to design Pandemic, which in turn helped inspire the many cooperative games published since. Leacock himself has also designed Forbidden Island, Forbidden Desert, and Forbidden Sky, a trio of cooperative games that are somewhat less complex than Pandemic but no less challenging. Other popular games in the genre include Robinson Crusoe, Chronicles of Crime, Hanabi, Spirit Island, Eldritch Horror, and Aeon's End (and Aeon's End Legacy). Any of those is a fantastic choice for a two-player game night, and you don't need more than the titles to see that cooperative games offer a wide variety of themes, making it easy to find at least one that will appeal to you and your playing partner.

One issue to be aware of with cooperative games is the possibility that a player with a strong personality can take too much control. The joy of a cooperative game is working together to achieve a joint victory; that joy can be greatly diminished by a player who decides to tell everyone else what moves they should make. It can be a delicate balance because discussing options with other players often leads to strategic revelations that would not have been discovered otherwise. Everyone playing a cooperative game needs to understand this and respect the fact that each person at the table has final say over their own game turns. Particularly when you're playing a two-player cooperative game, it's critical that both people feel like they're an integral part of the team.

Great Games for Two Players

CODENAMES: DUET

Two to four players
Designed by Vlaada Chvátil and Scot Eaton
Published by Czech Games Edition (2017)

This cooperative version of Codenames—a kind of Password for the modern age—works fabulously with two players but can accommodate more. Players use one-word clues to attempt to communicate a random set of target words found in a five-by-five grid of cards. A single clue could generate multiple correct answers, or it could cause your partner to guess one of the forbidden assassin words and lose the round in one fell swoop.

Players are limited in the number of clues they can give to find the target words, and a campaign-style scoring system allows them to progress across a map of the world while completing ever more difficult games. Using the same basic structure as the other Codenames games (which include editions for fans of Marvel, Disney, Harry Potter, and other pop culture franchises), the designers have created a fantastic experience that feels familiar and new at the same time.

I adore the original Codenames—which works well with players of all ages and backgrounds, as the clues only have to make sense to the person making the guesses—and Codenames: Duet is a terrific choice for your next two-player game night.

EXIT: THE GAME—
THE ABANDONED CABIN

One to six players
Designed by Inka Brand and Markus Brand
Published by Kosmos (2016)

Escape rooms have gone from being an interesting curiosity to a viral sensation—there's even a Red Bull Escape Room World Championship. Their popularity has given rise to a parallel deluge of single-use tabletop games that aim to replicate the escape room experience at your dining room table.

The Exit series of games (more than fifteen titles, including The Stormy Flight, The Haunted Roller Coaster, and The Cemetery of the Knight) is a consistently well-designed collection of escape room experiences for your home. Included in the box is everything you need to spend an hour or two fighting your way through a variety of puzzles connected by a story. You'll decode instructions, build devices to solve puzzles, peer at pictures looking for clues . . . all with the pressure of completing your mission as quickly as possible. Teams score based on how long it takes them to obtain victory and how many hints they used along the way.

The Abandoned Cabin is a good entry point for the Exit series, and each game is rated for difficulty (novice to expert), so you can choose those that would be most appropriate for your particular group of problem solvers. Note: while the game box recommends up to six players, experience suggests that four is likely to be a better maximum number of participants, and it's superb with two.

FORBIDDEN ISLAND

Two to four players
Designed by Matt Leacock
Published by Gamewright (2010)

In Forbidden Island, players embark on a harrowing search for four elemental treasures (the Crystal of Fire, the Statue of the Wind, the Ocean's Chalice, and the Earth Stone) created by an ancient civilization. Of course, it's not a simple archaeological expedition—the island is booby-trapped to begin sinking when anyone attempts to steal the treasures . . . and that's exactly what you're there to do.

On each turn of this cooperative game, you have three actions to move your piece across the island, collect the treasures, shore up the sinking parts of the island, and generally survive long enough for everyone to grab the last helicopter off the island. At the end of each turn, you draw cards—which can give you more abilities, but which might also increase the rate of flooding and sink more of the island.

There's only one way to win (get off the island with the four treasures), but there are lots of ways to lose: if the helicopter landing pad sinks, if one of your team doesn't survive, if you fail to recover all four treasures, or if the island floods completely.

The difficulty can be increased or decreased simply by changing the starting level of the water gauge; there's no need to use a convoluted alternative setup. Regardless of how many players are in the game, playing time is almost always thirty minutes.

The components are high quality—nice cards, great chunky tiles with evocative forbidden island artwork reminiscent of the computer game Myst, and nifty plastic treasures—all packaged in a cool-looking tin. Forbidden Island is the first in a trilogy of cooperative games from the designer of Pandemic. If you enjoy it, be sure to take a look at Forbidden Desert and Forbidden Sky.

SAGRADA

One to four players
Designed by Adrian Adamescu and Daryl Andrews
Published by Floodgate Games (2017)

The name of this game comes from Antoni Gaudí's stunning architectural masterpiece, Basílica de la Sagrada Família, in Barcelona. Players face the challenge of building stained-glass windows using colorful translucent dice selected from a common pool and placed into a personal gridded window.

There are restrictions: a die cannot be placed next to another die of the same color or with the same number of pips on its face. To add to the difficulty, each player chooses a window pattern card at the beginning of the game that determines a color or number that can only appear on certain spaces. Each game is different because scoring goals (both individual and shared) and special powers are randomly selected.

After ten rounds, scores are totaled and players compare their masterworks. Sagrada is charming and clever and a joy to play, but perhaps the thing that stands out most about it is how beautiful everyone's creations are when they're completed.

UNMATCHED:
BATTLE OF LEGENDS, VOLUME ONE

Two to four players
Designed by Rob Daviau and Justin D. Jacobson
Published by Restoration Games (2019)

Dramatic fights involving legendary figures from a jambalaya of eras await when you bring Unmatched to the table. This is truly a battle of legends as King Arthur can face off against Medusa, Sindbad, or Alice (of Wonderland fame). The excellent movement system gives each battle board its own personality and makes it easy to see at a glance which figures are in range of one another.

Each character (or team; Unmatched works with two or four players) has different strengths and weaknesses thanks to the meticulously designed card decks—you cannot play Medusa the same way as King Arthur and be successful. The production quality is top-notch with high-quality miniatures and a modern design that is both thematic and eye-catching.

Several expansions for Unmatched already exist—adding characters like Sherlock Holmes, Bruce Lee, Robin Hood, Bigfoot, Dracula, the Invisible Man, Dr. Jekyll and Mr. Hyde, InGen (from *Jurassic Park*), and raptors (also *Jurassic Park*) to the mix—and more (including characters from *Buffy the Vampire Slayer*) are planned.

Publisher Restoration Games specializes in revitalizing games that have been out of print for at least a decade. Unmatched is based on the *Star Wars* tie-in game Epic Duels. Although the *Star Wars* theme is gone, Daviau (who codesigned Epic Duels with Craig Van Ness) and the Restoration Games team have kept everything that made the original fun while also improving it in many ways.

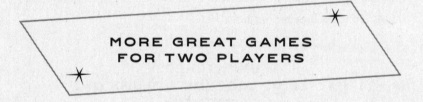

MORE GREAT GAMES FOR TWO PLAYERS

CROKINOLE
two or four players, public domain, 1876

JAIPUR
two players, designed by Sébastien Pauchon,
published by Asmodee, 2009

LOST CITIES
two players, designed by Reiner Knizia,
published by Kosmos, 1999

QWIRKLE
*two to four players, designed by Susan McKinley Ross,
published by Mindware, 2006*

TWILIGHT STRUGGLE
*two players, designed by Ananda Gupta and Jason Matthews,
published by GMT Games, 2005*

3

Small Group Game Nights
—three to six players—

I f I had to choose a favorite kind of game night, it would involve a small group of players gathered at someone's home. Game nights like this are more casual and relaxed than those with bigger groups, and everyone can play the same game so you don't have to worry about disrupting other tables—or being disrupted.

Small group nights with friends and close acquaintances are also some of the most common. These gatherings are fun, familiar, and generally lack the awkwardness that occasionally happens at larger gatherings. Sometimes, though, a small group might include a coworker you don't know very well, a friend of a friend who's a bit too obnoxious, or people you've never met before. The key to these smaller events—whether it's close friends at your home, coworkers in the office over lunch, or strangers in the Amtrak dining car—is the group chemistry. Everyone interacts with everyone at a small group game night; there's often no easy way to excuse yourself, or sit out, or see what another table is up to for a while. Any situation where one guest prevents the others from having a good time must be dealt with—or your game night will die. Perhaps more than any other type of game night, hosting a small group means being prepared to directly manage interpersonal dynamics.

WHO TO INVITE

As a host, it's easy to imagine that the success of your evening depends on choosing the right game—it is a *game* night, after all!—and it's easy to focus your attention on curating the perfect options. But there are no games without players, and the real secret to success is getting the right group together. As regular game-night host and guest Matt Carlson puts it, "Playing with the right friends is more important than playing the right game." Jeff Lingwall, who hosts a monthly game night at his home, offers this corollary: "Find a solid group of people who enjoy the same kind of games."

I won't soft-pedal it: deciding who to invite to your game night may be the biggest decision you make. When I was writing this book, more than one hundred people shared their game-night experiences with me via one-on-one interviews, Twitter, Facebook, BoardGameGeek, and other websites, and by far the most common piece of advice was to make sure the group dynamics work. Based on my own experience, I couldn't agree more. When a group clicks, everything is better. Games are chosen quickly. Explaining the rules goes smoothly. Laughs and smiles are constant. Game night becomes the night that everyone looks forward to because they know they'll be with good friends having a good time. Enjoying the game on the table is second nature when you already enjoy the company of the people you're playing with. My concept of the ideal gaming group may be different from yours, and that's to be expected. If you're planning to start a regular game night, focus on building a core group you and your friends are comfortable with.

Bruce Linsey, a longtime gamer who hosts game nights about once a month at his home or a local café, may have said it best: "Be selective about who you invite. Nothing can ruin the fun more quickly than someone who is unsporting or annoying to the others."

It's an unfortunate reality that some people are simply not fun to play games with. They might be wonderful, supportive friends. They might be your first choice for movie night or to try that new restaurant. But when the board comes out, they're too competitive or they tell everyone else what moves to make. They might think their rude jokes are funny when no one else does. Or perhaps they spend every waking hour repeating talking points from cable "news" shows on one end or the other of the political spectrum. (Ann Stolinsky, owner of Gontza Games, has wisely made her monthly game night "a politics-free zone.") Any behavior that disrupts your game night is something that you—the host—must tackle.

Christine Biancheria, who hosts weekly game nights at her home with her wife, Sue Frietsche, says creating a healthy group takes focused effort. "There's a lot of psychology in choosing whom to let in the group," she says. Ideally, she wants to play at least one game with someone before inviting them to game night.

Good advice, even if it's not always easy. Among the many factors you need to consider when developing a game group are what types of games your guests enjoy (e.g., strategy versus party, thirty-minute games versus two-hour games, etc.), how competitive they become while playing games, and how much they enjoy casual conversation during games. If half the people at your game night want to play Bunco and talk about the latest episode of *The Bachelor* and the other half is hoping to dive into a case of Portal Games' Detective, something has to give. As the host, one of your responsibilities is to prevent that kind of unnecessary tension.

Doing so requires careful thought about who you invite to game night. Spend time with the process of deciding. Make a list. Add names. Cross off names. Try not to invite people out of a sense of obligation. Sometimes that's unavoidable, but fight it where you can.

In *The Art of Gathering*, Priya Parker offers a lot of great advice that can apply to putting together any group at all, including the people you're going to host at game night. Among the most salient is her wisdom that "Particularly in smaller gatherings, every single person affects the dynamics of a group. . . . People who aren't fulfilling the purpose of your gathering are detracting from it, even if they do nothing to detract from it." In other words, everybody has to participate. This is especially true when the group is small, as many game nights are. If you have six people at your house and five of you are playing Sushi Go Party! but the sixth wanders around your living room browsing through your bookshelves, it will kill the vibe.

Even if everyone plays, it's important that they're all into the chosen game. Let's say you invite Sean, someone you've never met but he's the friend of a friend who swears that Sean loves board games. He arrives on game night and seems pleasant enough. Your group decides to play Time's Up! (a wonderful team game based on the public domain party game Celebrities). Great choice! Except Sean, it turns out, is completely not into pop culture. If he sits there and shrugs over and over, understanding few of the clues his partner gives, his discomfort will unintentionally make the game less fun for everyone else. And he's not having fun, either. Even if Sean loves board games like the robins love the worms in my front yard, he may not enjoy the kind of games your group plays.

Excluding people feels wrong. Of course it does. But as Josiah Fiscus says so well, "Liking board games should not be the only criteria for inviting someone." You're organizing game night to have fun, and sometimes the best way to do that is to exclude someone whose behavior or taste in games will prevent other guests from enjoying themselves. By carefully managing the invitation list, you are doing your job to foster a welcoming, fun, friendly, and safe environment for your guests.

One last thing: while you don't have to invite Sean, let me be abundantly clear that excluding people should never be done to diminish diversity. In her book, Parker addresses this seeming incongruity head-on. "Isn't exclusion, however thoughtful or intentional, the enemy of diversity? It is not." She advocates for what she calls "generous exclusion" as a way to ensure that diversity is "heightened and sharpened, rather than diluted in a hodgepodge of people," and we would do well to adopt this mindset for game nights. Her point is that an overly inclusive event—one that, say, included a group of people from diverse backgrounds (good) but who don't share anything in common when it comes to choosing board games (bad)—can be counterproductive. In the context of a game night, this means everyone should be on the same page about the style of game and intensity of play. Playing board games is a fun, easy, inclusive way to get to know new people and can be an effective tool in building diverse communities.

I encourage you to always invite new blood to the table—whether that's having a friends-of-friends night, including a coworker, or inviting a newcomer at your church or the parents of the new kid at school. These are all natural opportunities to widen your circle of gaming friends. As we discussed in chapter 2, games are a way for us to share experiences, to strengthen our social ties and relationships, and to understand one another better. The only way our hobby will continue to grow is by embracing newcomers of diverse backgrounds as players, designers, and publishers. Many gamers welcome newbies with open arms. Unfortunately, that's not universally true. I've been to far too many game events that lacked diversity. I believe the boardgaming community has taken some steps forward in recent years, but much progress remains to be made. You and I can help by ensuring diversity—by practicing Parker's generous exclusion—at our own game nights.

INTERPERSONAL DYNAMICS

Host enough game nights and you'll eventually see a wildly elevated level of competitiveness, out-and-out anger, or any of a dozen other inappropriate reactions.

Bonnie Winston, the matchmaker we spoke to in chapter 2, has seen this play out rather dramatically in real life. "Back in the mid '90s, I had a boyfriend from Bay Ridge, Brooklyn," she says. "My boyfriend and his friends used to have one night a month where they played board games. One time they were playing Monopoly with cousins, one guy named Mike. Mike had Park Place, another player had the opportunity to buy Boardwalk, and a heated fight broke out. Well, Mike pulled out his 'piece' . . . his gun! Needless to say, he won." (Also needless to say, Mike should never be invited back to game night.)

Thankfully, not every Monopoly disagreement ends with the brandishing of firearms. Search for "crying during Monopoly" on YouTube, and one of the things you'll find is a video of a young boy reacting after he landed on the Income Tax space. A woman, displaying what some child psychologists would refer to as "poor judgment," decided this was the moment to turn on a video camera. "Where's all your money gone, buddy?" she asks. "Taxes," he says before starting to sob. The woman tries to console him by saying it's part of the game, but the boy will have none of it. "It's not fun," he says between tears. "It's the worst part of the game." As "worst parts of the game" go, Monopoly's Income Tax space is pretty tame. Land on the space and you must choose whether to pay $200 or 10 percent of the total value of your assets. (Some modern versions of Monopoly eliminate the 10 percent option.) Since the space is not far past Go, chances are good you just collected $200 anyway so the net effect should never be too damaging.

The classic real estate game certainly engenders its fair share of dramatic reactions. Other YouTube videos include "Kid Playing Monopoly Goes Insane," "Monopoly Kid (original video)," and "Funny Monopoly Meltdown." Not to mention "Angry Gamer Wrecks Monopoly," "Psycho Kid Rage at Monopoly," and "Greatest Monopoly Freakout Ever." But please trust me when I say it's not worth watching those videos. I've done that hard work so you don't have to.

The point is that games can cause hurt feelings, and Monopoly is not the only one that brings out strong emotions. Mark Jackson and his wife have been married nearly thirty years and they've played plenty of games together. But one early game didn't go so well. "We can laugh about it now, but when we were dating, I bought her a portable backgammon board and replaced all of the pieces with Hershey's Kisses for Valentine's Day," he says. "Sometime during the evening, we got in a fight and she left, so I ate all the pieces. For our twenty-fifth wedding anniversary, I replaced the pieces in the same travel backgammon set again. This time, we shared."

One obvious, yet too often overlooked, way to reduce the possibility of hard feelings is to choose a game everyone is likely to enjoy. "You don't want to force people into playing something they won't like," says Mark Hager. "When I was younger, I tried to talk people into trying games, but now if they say they won't like it, I let it go. If someone says, 'I'm *willing* to play,' that's a bad sign."

"Certain games lend themselves to the likelihood of bad feelings," says Josiah Fiscus. To help protect against unnecessary conflict or hurt feelings, "some expectation management should go into teaching that kind of a game." For example, when you're playing a game like Survive: Escape from Atlantis!—in which players move sharks so that they eat other players' pawns—he recommends telling people up front, "Hey, this is a mean game, so people will pick on you if you're perceived to be in the lead."

While I love the classic negotiation-and-backstabbing game Diplomacy (which I'll discuss in more detail later in this chapter) and have played a few dozen games without a single bruise (unless you count the lasting damage that's been done to my ego since I've never won), that's not the case for everyone. "About six hours into a game of seven-player Diplomacy, a few of the less hardy souls decided another hour would be enough, with the leader at that point declared the victor," says Bob

Schwartz, the former owner of Games Unlimited in Pittsburgh. "Soon thereafter, one player broke a game-long alliance by attacking a previous ally. When I say the offended party came across the board and table, I'm not exaggerating. With game pieces flying everywhere, the other players soon broke up the altercation. Now forty years later, the two have never spoken to each other since."

Some games include thematic or narrative elements that some players won't be comfortable with. The theme of Lifeboats, for example, can turn people off. In the game, players struggle to survive after a boating accident. At various times during the game, players vote on which lifeboat will spring a leak and which of the meeples in that boat will be thrown overboard.

But it doesn't have to be the entire game that makes players squirm. In Catan, one of the most popular games in the world, the robber pawn prevents any resources from being produced by whatever tile it's on. When you roll a seven, you must move it to a new tile. Some players can't bring themselves to put the robber on a tile that will affect someone else. Instead, they move it somewhere that looks unlikely to hurt anyone's production.

In another well-regarded game, Citadels, each player chooses one of eight characters. Among them are an assassin, who "kills" another character and prevents that player from taking a turn, and a thief, who steals gold. Mihail Mikov says his girlfriend "is a pure care bear" and playing Citadels isn't something she enjoyed. "She didn't want to attack others and felt real bad when she got attacked," he says. "She finished the game with tears in her eyes. I really regret causing her the pain."

DEALING WITH PROBLEMATIC GUESTS

In 2010, give or take a year or two, Edward (not his real name) was in therapy for post-traumatic stress disorder, a condition marked by, among other things, hypervigilance, an increased startle response, flashbacks, and panic attacks. His therapist encouraged him to engage in more social settings and knew he enjoyed board games. She suggested that he attend a local meetup for gamers and he agreed.

Before the games began, while everyone was introducing themselves and making small talk, Edward arrived and found a good place to stand. Another guy entered and slammed the door behind him. The loud noise caused Edward to react both visibly, with a start, and audibly, with a yelp. The man who came in noticed, laughed, and said, "Scared you, didn't I?"

If it had ended there, the man's comment could be written off as an obnoxious, but not entirely outrageous, response. But he wouldn't let it go. A few minutes later, the man moved next to Edward and yelled, "How you doin'?" Edward dropped the plate he was holding, dumping chips and salsa on the floor. While Edward cleaned up the mess, the man kept pushing. He laughed again, asked Edward what was wrong with him, and told him he needed to chill out.

Furious, Edward moved to another room. He wound up playing Agricola, a deep strategy game that can take about two hours. Halfway through the game, the same man came up behind Edward, grabbed his shoulders, and yelled. Edward shouted in surprise and pretty much knocked over his board. He got up and apologized to the table for quitting, but he had to leave. Because of that experience, Edward says, he gave up on trying to be social for several years—to him, it wasn't worth it.

As a host, you're responsible for the well-being of your guests. Edward's experience highlights how important it is to be aware of everything that's happening at your game night. Inviting the right people to game night in the first place is key, but try as you might there will probably come a time when you have to uninvite someone, either because they don't jell with the group or because they repeatedly act in unacceptable ways, like the person who thought it was funny to startle Edward.

Being the enforcer is a job few people want. But if you're the person organizing and hosting a game night, it falls to you. Whether it's a player who doesn't know how to lose (or win) graciously, someone who constantly stares at their phone during games, or the friend of a friend who doesn't have enough respect for personal space, you have to step in—even and *especially* with friends.

Problematic behavior is often easiest to address if you're the direct recipient. Take, for example, my experience during a game of Power Grid. The goal of this game by Friedemann Friese is to supply cities with power. Players bid against one another to purchase power plants that use various fuels, such as garbage, coal, and wind, to generate the power needed by the cities on the board. Skilled players can move through the early rounds fairly quickly, but I was slow to get on the Power Grid bandwagon. I played it once soon after its release in 2004, but it took a couple of years before I had the chance to play again. At my second play I was still very much a novice, and everyone else at the table was far more experienced. As I considered my first move, the player to my right grew impatient. After half a minute or so, he said, essentially, "Well, clearly on your first move you're going to do this and this," and proceeded to do those things on my behalf. It was neither advice, nor a suggestion, nor a helpful hint. He told me, directly, what actions I must take and then took them. It was baffling and irksome to say the least, but wanting to be a good sport, I nodded politely and said, "I think that's right."

After the same thing happened on my second turn, I took a different approach. I turned to the player and calmly said, "I appreciate that you know this game far better than I do, and I appreciate that you want to speed things up. If you'd like me to step out and find another game, I'm happy to do that. Otherwise, I'll be making my own moves from here on out." He seemed surprised, as though it had never occurred to him that his actions would be considered rude. He said something along the lines of "Sure, of course." The game proceeded without any further incident, that player and I got along well, and I had a good time despite finishing in last place.

Problems in small groups can range from relatively minor ("know-it-alls and loudmouths" as one person described them) to criminal. Having to deal with the latter at a home game night is rare, but you're likely to need to address the former at some point. The people you've invited to game night should *always* feel safe and respected. If one player appears to be harassing, bullying, or intimidating another, you should handle the situation immediately.

In many circumstances, the best first step is to have a one-on-one conversation with the player on the receiving end of the behavior to see how they view what happened. If they're not comfortable, or you can see that the behavior is making other players uncomfortable, it's perfectly appropriate to encourage the guest causing the discomfort to tone it down. "Don't be afraid to confront a person ruining other people's experiences," says gamer Pete Evans. "Often they don't know they're doing it." You can take the offender aside, describe the situation, and tell them politely but directly, "I'm sorry, but we don't do that at this game night." Make it clear that the admonition is coming from you, the host. Don't lay it off on your other guests.

If the behavior continues, you might choose to strengthen your warning. But you may quickly arrive at a point many hosts have had to deal with: disinviting the offender. Take solace in the fact that you are not alone. It's been done before, many thousands of times. And it will be done again. The simplest way to disinvite someone is to remove them from your email list or group text. Of course, this approach is an awful lot like ghosting so depending on your relationship with the person, a more direct conversation may be needed. If so, be candid but kind. Perhaps, "I'm sorry, but it seems like our game group is not a great fit for you." Those approaches will solve nearly any issue. In more extreme situations, you might consider letting everyone know that you're taking a break from hosting game night—and then bring it back online, slowly at first, rebuilding your guest list from scratch.

All that said, be careful not to pull the plug too soon. Jim Carvin, who hosts regular game nights at his church and a larger game day every year on Black Friday, tries to give people time to fit in. "Though it may be tempting to exclude people who don't perfectly meld with the group, it's a shortsighted mistake," he says. "Take the time to cultivate those once-a-month or once-a-week friendships and enjoy the camaraderie—because that's what this is really all about."

PLAYING TO WIN VS. PLAYING FOR THE EXPERIENCE

I'm a member of Generation X, and my family's collection of board games in the 1970s and 1980s didn't contain any surprises. Our game shelves were filled with titles like Monopoly, Risk, Sorry!, Connect 4, and Battleship. Boy, did we have some fights during those games!

Thinking back, some of the reasons for the fights are clear. (First and foremost, my little sister was always wrong whenever we disagreed on something, but that's a whole nother book.) In Monopoly and Risk, the goal is not simply to improve your own position; you must also completely eliminate every other player from the game. Nothing short of total annihilation will do. In Sorry!, good strategy dictates that you will often send your opponents' pieces back to their starting points, destroying their hard-won progress. (And you will never, *never* apologize for doing so, at least not sincerely.) Both Connect 4 and Battleship are one-on-one contests. When played by an eight-year-old boy and his seven-year-old sister, it's not difficult to anticipate some . . . well, let's go with "vocal disagreements."

Ironically, the game that taught me to enjoy the experience of the game itself more than winning is one notorious for destroying friend-ships: Diplomacy. Many stories about Diplomacy end with "And we never played another game together again." But iron sharpens iron, and sometimes the longest-lasting lessons are those that are forged in fire.

Diplomacy, set in pre–World War I Europe, is a pure negotiation game. Each player takes on the role of a specific country: Great Britain, France, Austria-Hungary, Germany, Italy, Russia, or Turkey. Players spend several minutes negotiating in private at the start of each round, then write specific orders to move their army and navy units across the board. There's absolutely no requirement that you honor any commit-ments made during the negotiations, and that's why Diplomacy can easily descend into bitterness. Some people don't react well to being lied to, even in a game where that's necessary and expected.

Playing Diplomacy with my high school buddies John and Chuck, plus Chuck's older brother, Jim, was fantastic. Jim crushed us the first time we played, and Chuck, John, and I all understood immediately that we had to work together or Jim would continue to win time after time. So in game after game, we did exactly that: we worked together. Right up until the moment when Jim convinced one of us that he was out of the game, there was no way he could win, and he only wanted to help that person win instead. You can tell where this is going, right? Jim always hoodwinked one of us, shattering the supposedly unbreak-able Alliance of Three and causing us to fight among ourselves while he marched to victory.

Diplomacy takes about six hours to play so if you're not enjoying the experience of the game, there's no way to have a good time. And if your competitive juices flow so strongly that winning is the only thing that matters, Diplomacy will almost always be a miserable experience—for you *and* everyone you're playing with. For that matter, most games will be a miserable experience with a win-at-all-costs attitude.

Looking back, Jim did me a real favor by so thoroughly demolishing us in those games of Diplomacy. He taught me that it's possible to have fun playing even if you don't win in the end. But if we ever play Diplomacy again, revenge will be mine.

SEATING ARRANGEMENTS

Over the course of playing thousands of games, I can't recall seating order being discussed more than a handful of times. And yet it can have a big impact in at least two ways. First, some games have a first-player advantage. That is, the first player to take a turn benefits by being able to place their tokens, select cards, or take some other action before any other player is able to do so. The best-known example of a first-player advantage is chess, where white takes the first turn and has been shown to win in tournament games between 52 and 56 percent of the time. However, most modern games have been designed to account for any first-player advantage (for example, by giving later players extra money) so this typically isn't anything to be concerned about.

The more salient issue with seating order is who sits next to whom. In many games, players can make a move that mostly benefits themselves or one that mostly harms an opponent. In Ticket to Ride, for example, if it looks like an opponent is trying to connect St. Louis to Atlanta, you can easily claim the one-train connection between Nashville and Atlanta to force them to use at least seven trains to accomplish what could have been done with three. Any player can do that, but it stings the most if the person on your right—the player taking the turn immediately before yours—does it. Couples tend to sit next to each other, and some people simply won't make a move that hurts their partner, which is sweet but also affects everyone else at the table.

If this happens at your game nights, try changing the seating arrangement so that couples aren't next to each other. I'm willing to bet it generates a different dynamic. There are several ways to accomplish this. The free app Chwazi, popular among gamers, is designed to randomly choose a start player, but it can also determine seating order. After the start player is chosen, use the app again—excluding the start player—to determine who takes the second seat and then continue until all the seats are filled. (Chwazi can also randomly assign teammates in team-based games like Codenames.) Alternatively, you could have the players roll dice (a twenty-sided die is perfect for this job) with the highest roll taking the first seat, the next highest taking the second, and so on. And if you want to be absolutely sure that certain people aren't next to each other, set out place cards in advance so everyone knows exactly where to sit.

GAME-FRIENDLY FOOD AND DRINK

It's game night. Guests will arrive soon, but you're ready. The $200 Kickstarter edition of the hottest new board game is on the table, and you know the rules inside and out. Your friends are going to love it. Also on the table: bowls overflowing with cheese puffs and various greasy snacks, glasses filled to the rim with red wine, and absolutely no napkins or coasters . . .

You wake up in a cold sweat.

Thank heaven, it's only a nightmare.

And you should *never* let this nightmare become a reality.

If you ask a certain group of my friends, they'll tell you that there was a night when a single, half-full glass of water was knocked over while we were playing games, that the water traveled (like a roaring river in my memory) toward a few cards, and that I jumped out of my chair and threw my body in front of the water to save the cards while screaming "*Nooooooo!*" like the hero in a bad 1980s action movie. They'll tell you that I was willing to put my own well-being at risk to save those cards far more readily than I ever would to save any of them.

And I will not disagree with any of those points.

Thankfully, most games can be easily replaced, and many game publishers have customer-friendly parts replacement policies (although that's beginning to change as larger companies acquire smaller companies). But while I will happily debate anyone on the cost-benefit ratio of board games versus nearly any other form of entertainment, games aren't cheap. Catan and Ticket to Ride, two of the most popular games in the world, sell for about forty-five dollars each. Naturally, people like to take care of their games, and for good reason: if you treat it right, a game can last for decades.

Because cards are perhaps the component most vulnerable to damage, some players buy plastic sleeves to protect them. A number of game publishers list the type of card sleeves a game needs on the back of the box. Veteran gamer Chuck Ledger knows how important sleeves can be. "Two experienced gamers wanted to learn Dominion," he says. "I taught them the game. When I returned, they were eating barbecue fried chicken with their fingers. The cards actually stuck together when they tried to shuffle. Boy was I glad that I sleeve my cards!"

The best protection for board games, though, is the simplest: don't touch any part of a game if your fingers are coated with food grease, cheese powder residue, or anything similar. If you're eating and drinking at the game table, have plenty of napkins nearby. A few moist towelettes wouldn't be a bad idea either. And for the love of all that is good and holy, whenever possible give each player their own bottled beverage. With a lid.

If wine is involved, you may want to provide sippy cups. (Yes, this is a real thing: sippy cups designed specifically for wine do exist. To make them sound classier, you can refer to them as "wine glasses with a drink-through lid.") "We were playing my first copy of Filthy Rich at a New Year's Eve gathering of friends," says Mark Jackson. "The now ex-wife of one of them had a glass of red wine and ignored my request to keep it away from the game—basically saying that I was a nervous Nellie. Five minutes later, she knocked the wine across all the cards. Red wine does not pair well with cards." Mark didn't say whether the wine incident contributed to the end of the marriage, but I think it's safe to assume.

Kevin Wilson, designer of games like Descent, Fury of Dracula, and Batman: The Animated Series Adventures, has also suffered the wrath of red wine. "A tipsy playtester once spilled a full glass of red wine into the box holding one of my prototypes," he says. "After a moment of silence, some of the pieces started floating on top of the wine, which was miraculously held in by the box. They were very apologetic, and I just made a new copy of the prototype, but man, there was nothing salvageable from that copy. I even threw away the card sleeves."

Of course, wine is far from the only offender. Frank Branham once accidentally dumped a large container of Gulab jamun on someone else's copy of Hare and Tortoise. "That trashed it," he says. "These are Indian donuts soaked in rose sugar syrup. Tasty, but not a board game topping." At BoardGameGeek, a GeekList created by Chris Tannhauser and titled "Snacktastrophe: When Games + Food = Big Fat Man-Tears" documents dozens of additional disasters. I'd love to see the Blumhouse film version of that GeekList.

If it's your game being played, think about all of this in advance. Don't bring your irreplaceable War of the Ring Collector's Edition (one copy sold on BoardGameGeek for $1,500) to game night if you're not 100 percent confident that the players will treat it with the care it deserves. On the flip side, don't freak out if someone gets a little grease on one of the cards in a twenty-dollar game.

"My view," says Josiah Fiscus, "is that, in the same way that you would be generous to your guests with your food, drinks, electricity, running water, etc., you should also be generous with the general depreciation your components will experience from being handled." He considers each of his games to be a long-term consumable item along the lines of an appliance, something that will eventually need to be replaced. "Viewing games that way, rather than as family heirlooms, will make you happier in the long run," he says.

Some people avoid potential disaster by refusing to mix game night with food. At all. Steve from Alexandria, Virginia, has a very simple philosophy: "Food shouldn't be the focus of a game night." He's not alone in his allegiance to food-free game nights, although far more people seem to enjoy making a meal or providing snacks for their guests to munch on. Favorite gaming snacks include pretzels, popcorn, M&Ms, cookies, and brownies, along with healthy alternatives like celery sticks, carrots, grapes, and nuts.

If you do prepare a meal for game night, using a slow cooker is a terrific option since you can start the food before you leave for work and it will be ready in time for your guests to arrive. But if cooking's not your thing, many gaming groups order out for dinner. Vanessa Shannen-Anderson has an additional rule for roleplaying games: the Dungeon Master, who runs the campaign, never pays for food or drink. "They've done so much work, hours and hours of prep. I can chip in for their meal at the very least!"

GAME-NIGHT COCKTAILS

If you enjoy the occasional adult beverage, game night presents a great opportunity to try new cocktail recipes. When it comes to liquor, I'm mostly a whiskey neat sort of guy—although I do have fond memories of drinking mai tais with my wife when we visited Hawaii. Which brings me to a key point: cocktails on game night are probably best when they relate to the game being played. So if you're taking Greg Daigle's underrated 2011 gem Hawaii off your shelf, that's the perfect time to bring out the rum and set the atmosphere with a few mai tais of your own. Also required: those little paper umbrellas.

Actor Rich Sommer, perhaps best known as Harry Crane on *Mad Men* but seen more recently on the CW show *In the Dark*, is a big fan of both board games and cocktails. A few years back, he hosted a podcast called *Cardboard!*, on which he often recommended drinks to go along with certain games. Rich's recommendations included a gin-based drink known as Corpse Reviver No. 2 when playing Dead of Winter (it would also work well with Zombicide or Last Night on Earth—any zombie-themed game, for that matter), a whiskey-based drink called Rusty Six-Shooter for Colt Express (that one would be great with other western-themed games, too, especially Bang!), and a creation known as a Drambuie Smoke-N-Milk to go with Formula D as a nod to the Indy 500's tradition of giving the winner a bottle of milk.

On the GeekList "Board Game Cocktails," gamers have put together a nice catalog of cocktail suggestions. My personal favorite is the Wooly Mitten, a mix of Southern Comfort, peppermint schnapps, and Baileys Irish cream, when playing Ticket to Ride: Nordic Countries. I'd also give that drink a shot with the dogsled race game Snow Tails or Carcassonne: Winter Edition.

The possibilities go on: Pair a classic Manhattan with Andreas Seyfarth's 1994 classic board game Manhattan. Sip on a grog (dark rum, lime juice, and brown sugar) while enjoying Merchants & Marauders, a game many consider the best pirate-themed game ever released. Or enjoy a Moscow Mule during a game of Dual Powers: Revolution 1917, a terrific 2018 game designed by Brett Myers.

If you're playing Sherlock Holmes: Consulting Detective (or any of the other many Sherlock-themed games), Todd Robinson, an acclaimed crime fiction author and a bartender at Shade in New York City, recommends a Brandy Alexander. The cognac-based drink was created around the turn of the twentieth century, the same era when

Sir Arthur Conan Doyle's famous detective was captivating audiences across the globe. Eryk Pruitt, author of Southern noir and co-owner of Yonder Bar in Hillsborough, North Carolina, says one of his favorite mysterious drinks is The Conquistador, a mix of aged rum, lime juice, amaro, and Mexican cream.

And if you think a game with any complexity wouldn't pair well with a cocktail or two, take the advice Chelsea Davis offers to readers at Forbes.com: prepare a Sugar Plum Fairy, complete with rum, Irish cream, and sherry, and then sit down at the table for . . . Candyland.

If beer is more to your liking, visit the Opinionated Gamers website to read Tery Noseworthy's article "Opinionated Drinkers, Quarantine Gaming Edition," focusing on great beers to pair with board games. Her suggestions include pairing the game Blackout Hong Kong with Brooklyn Brewing's Black Ops Stout, the game Seasons with Honest Weight's Odd Seasons Belgian IPA, and the game Las Vegas with Night Shift Brewing's Chance the DIPA.

Your imagination is the only limit on what cocktails—or other drinks (Viticulture with a bottle of red wine, anyone?)—can work at game night. Experiment and enjoy!

On a serious note, serving alcohol or allowing your guests to bring their own alcohol gives you a new set of issues to be aware of. Joe Cook, who hosts regular poker nights, remembers one time when "a first-timer had too much to drink, curled up in a ball in the dog's bed on the floor, and passed out. It happened so quickly, we thought he had a heart attack or something!" If someone appears to be intoxicated, you should never allow them to drive, and some states have social host liability laws that determine when a host can be held liable if they serve alcohol to someone who goes on to drive under the influence. It's always a good idea to help people who may have had too much to drink find a taxi or an Uber or a place where they can spend the night.

Great Games for Small Groups

THE CREW:
THE QUEST FOR PLANET NINE

Two to five players
Designed by Thomas Sing
Published by Kosmos (2019)

The Crew is a compact box of cooperative trick-taking dynamite. If you enjoy classic card games like Spades and Hearts, get it onto your game table.

Players work together to send missions into space. As in Spades, one player leads a card and the others must follow suit. The high card wins the trick and starts the next trick. The twist here is that completing missions involves meeting specific objectives each round, such as having particular players take tricks with a specific card in them or keeping one of the players from taking any tricks. The game includes a logbook that lays out the story and details the fifty missions to be completed.

This would be all too easy if players could talk about their hands, so there are strict communication rules. Deciding when the time is right to play a card in front of you and "radio" your fellow astronauts is one of many interesting challenges along the way to finishing your quest for Planet Nine.

PARKS

One to five players
Designed by Henry Audubon
Published by Keymaster Games (2019)

You won't find a more beautifully produced or wonderfully illustrated board game than Parks. Everything inside the box is easy to look at and fun to handle. The game itself is a delight to play, an enchanting romp through some of the grandest national parks in the United States.

Each player controls a pair of hikers on four seasonal walks through the parks. You choose from various actions on your turn, balancing the number of actions you want to take each season with how far you want to travel on the trail. When an opponent occupies the space you had your eye on, you're forced to either use your campfire (allowing you to put a hiker on an already taken spot) or pick another space. The choices become increasingly difficult.

In each season, players collect resources from the board to pay for park cards, which feature amazing artwork depicting the national parks. Like any good visit to a park, taking pictures is also essential. Victory points are represented by photos and postcards from your journey.

You may never get to experience every national park in real life, but with Parks you can probably get close.

TICKET TO RIDE

Two to five players
Designed by Alan R. Moon
Published by Days of Wonder (2004)

Ticket to Ride is one of my favorite games, and I'm far from alone. Nearly ten million copies of the games in the Ticket to Ride series have been sold, making it one of the most popular modern board games. The original Ticket to Ride, featuring a game board that's a map of the United States and southern Canada, perfectly blends smart game design and social fun. The quality of the production helped set a new standard for board games.

Part of the appeal is how easy it is to teach. You can do one of three things on your turn: select two train cards, play a set of cards to connect two cities, or take more destination tickets. When one player has two or fewer trains remaining, each player gets a final turn and the game is over. Players score for connecting cities and for completing tickets—with uncompleted tickets counting against their score.

Playing with three or five players is much more cutthroat than playing with two or four because restrictions on which routes are available make the board more crowded. Regardless of the number of players, the game moves quickly and is filled with tension and excitement.

Many additional versions, each with its own map, have been created since the first Ticket to Ride was published—two of my favorites are Pennsylvania and Nordic Countries. Certain maps are best for smaller player counts (Switzerland and India, for example) while others offer unique challenges (such as Asia's team version and the global scope of Rails & Sails).

WINGSPAN

One to five players
Designed by Elizabeth Hargrave
Published by Stonemaier Games (2019)

Wingspan is one of the most award-winning titles of recent years, earning considerable praise for its clever gameplay and stunning artwork. In this family-friendly and educational game, you take on the role of a bird enthusiast, researching and observing our winged friends in their natural habitats. Each of the 170 lavishly illustrated bird cards shows a different species, along with a variety of fun facts.

The goal is to collect birds, earning points and special abilities. On your turn, you can either play a bird card out of your hand, gain food (which you need to play the bird cards), lay eggs (which are worth points at the end of the game), or draw more bird cards. Each action is associated with a habitat, and when you take the action, you activate all of the previously played birds that live there.

The game has an engine-building aspect, meaning a player's earlier actions give them special abilities and more powerful turns later in the game. Engine building is popular among game enthusiasts, and part of what makes Wingspan special is how it implements this system in an easy-to-understand manner.

Between the impressive production value—a model birdhouse is used to roll dice—and delightful gameplay, Wingspan is sure to be a hit at game night. Along the way, you may find yourself learning more about birds than you ever anticipated.

WITS & WAGERS

Three to seven players
Designed by Dominic Crapuchettes
Published by North Star Games (2005)

If you were alive in the 1980s, you remember that guy who wanted to play Trivial Pursuit so he could show off how much more he knew than everyone else in the room. To be clear, we all hated that guy.

But what if you could play a trivia game where the questions were offbeat enough that no one could be expected to know the precise answer? (For example, "How many Pringles come in a standard-size can?") And what if, after everyone revealed their guesses, you could bet on which one was right for extra points?

Welcome to Wits & Wagers. There are seven rounds, one question per round. Every answer is a number. Players write their answers on little dry-erase boards, which are placed on the game board from lowest to highest. Players then bet on which answer they think is right. The closest answer (without going over—thanks, Bob Barker!) pays out according to the odds on the board.

I've been a big fan of Wits & Wagers since the original version was released more than fifteen years ago. Later editions have improved the already solid gameplay and added new questions. It's the perfect trivia game for people who thought they hated trivia games.

MORE GREAT GAMES FOR SMALL GROUPS

AZUL
two to four players, designed by Michael Kiesling,
published by Next Move Games, 2017

JUST ONE
three to seven players, designed by Ludovic Roudy and Bruno Sautter,
published by Repos Productions, 2018

THE MIND
two to four players, designed by Wolfgang Warsch,
published by Pandasaurus Games, 2018

OCEANS
two to four players, designed by Nick Bentley, Dominic Crapuchettes,
Ben Goldman, and Brian O'Neill, published by North Star Games, 2020

TERRAFORMING MARS
one to five players, designed by Jacob Fryxelius,
published by Stronghold Games, 2016

Large Group Game Nights
—seven to ten players—

Adozen or so years ago, a weekly game gathering started up at a restaurant close to where I work. I wasn't acquainted with any of the organizers personally, but I'm always interested in playing games and meeting others who love the hobby. I attended their game nights three or four times, and every time I was clearly the odd man out. When I walked in at the announced starting time or a few minutes after, everyone was already sitting at a table and either playing a game or halfway through explaining the rules.

They all clearly knew one another, but nobody seemed to be in charge and nobody introduced themselves to the new guy. The result was that people who didn't know anyone else (like me) were left to fend for themselves. The gamers weren't actively unfriendly, but they certainly weren't friendly, either.

By contrast, more recently I took part in a number of game nights at a makerspace in Dillsburg, Pennsylvania. The organizer, Jared Vento, does a remarkable job of ensuring that everyone who attends feels welcome and included. He greets newcomers, gives them a brief tour of the facility, and introduces them to a table of gamers where they can join right in. He does all this despite the fact that it means he's less able to join games, he has to keep an eye out for anyone new who comes in, and when he does play a game, people often interrupt him to ask questions.

Jared's open and welcoming attitude filters down to all of the regulars at his game days. He's in charge, so he sets the tone—whether intentionally or not. Others naturally look to the leader of a group and emulate that person's example. Bear that in mind, especially if you host game days with seven or more players and double-especially if you host game days that large that are open to the public. You'll need to spend a lot of energy on activities like greeting people, organizing game tables, and checking on your guests—activities that don't involve actually playing a game. If you're not okay with that, you should probably stick to smaller events.

ENLISTING HELP

Just like Santa Claus delegates the actual toy-building process to his elves and Felonius Gru trusts his minions (well, sort of trusts them) to handle major parts of his schemes, success at a large game night can depend on your support team. Having an assistant or two at the ready will often prove useful. If your game night is a big group of longtime friends, this probably isn't necessary, but you never know when you might need an extra set of hands. This could be as simple as asking someone to monitor the chips and make sure no one has filled their red Kool-Aid to the brim, to watch for any garbage or recycling that needs to be dealt with, and to scan the room for any game pieces that escape from their boxes. If you're running a game night with several new attendees, your assistants can play the role of the Welcome Wagon and see that newcomers get involved in a game.

That warmth and welcome can make a big difference in your guests' experience. Nicola, who lives in Derby, UK, has hosted game nights in various locations, including at local pubs and cafés. She recommends "having someone at hand to meet and greet and break down barriers for people, get them joined in a game without them feeling intrusive." That last point is often overlooked: Many people, especially when they're joining a gathering for the first time, will hesitate to inject themselves into a game. They need an affirmative invitation.

"We always try and make everyone feel welcome," says Rick Parker of the Sheffield Board Games Club in the UK. The club actively seeks new attendees by advertising its events on Facebook. Some keys to creating a welcoming environment, Rick says, are "a regular venue and members willing to answer questions and help greet newcomers."

If you have several tables of games going at once, as happens at larger gatherings, it's also critical to have multiple people who can explain game rules. It's best to know who they will be in advance—appointing them, if necessary—so they can prepare (head back to chapter 1 for some tips).

SPLITTING INTO SMALLER GROUPS

Once a game night reaches six or seven people, the question will inevitably come up: Should we all play together, or should we split into two groups? As the host, you need to be ready to answer that question—and there will be people with strong feelings on each side.

For some, game night is primarily a social experience. The point is to gather with friends and enjoy their company. Playing games happens to be an entertaining means to this end, so dividing the group into multiple tables can be seen as antithetical to the purpose of the evening. For others, games are the focus and being able to spend time with people whose company you enjoy is a pleasant by-product. Still others may be much more comfortable interacting with a smaller group than a larger one.

You'll know what's right for your group because you already

thought about this back when you developed your invitation list, right? If your guests can be described as *game first*, chances are they'll be most comfortable splitting into smaller groups. On the other hand, *social first* guests will likely want to stay together and find a game that everyone can play. The first few times this situation arises, a little trial and error may be in order. If the group's preference doesn't become clear after two or three game nights, ask people what they prefer, but do so individually—not in front of the group, because in that circumstance some people will provide whatever answer they think the group desires, not what they themselves would want.

Ian Campbell, who lives in Helsinki, says that if you do have a larger group all play the same game it's "important to have a backup game for folks who get bounced early so they're not just sitting around." He's right. If you're playing a game where some players will be eliminated before the game ends, have a plan in place so they can quickly get into another game.

Meanwhile, more than four thousand miles away in Minnesota, Jeremy Thigpen's group tends to take the other approach. "Anytime we hit six or more players, we usually split into two smaller groups," he says. "Half might want to play a deck-builder and half might want to play a Eurogame. Perfect! We can make that happen."

There's no objectively right or wrong answer to the question of whether you should split into smaller groups. Consider all the factors and make the best decision you can. You can always take the other route at your next game night.

INTRODUCING NEW GAMES TO NON-GAMERS

One of my favorite things about this hobby is teaching new games to people who don't have any experience with modern board games, people whose first thought when they're asked to name a game is *Monopoly*. Seeing someone discover the joy of playing beautiful games like Qwirkle, Sagrada, and Azul is wonderful to behold.

When introducing novices to new games—which works well in large groups because you can do it at a table with either many players or just a few, whichever makes the newbie more comfortable—it's a good idea to choose titles that are minimally complex and capture their attention quickly. Nicola from the UK points out that one of the host's responsibilities is to have a range of games available, "particularly filler games and family games because the gamers will always bring the bigger, heavier, longer games to play."

Greg Clensy, who hosts a monthly game night at his house, is an old pro at teaching neophytes. Among the games he uses are For Sale ("People always love this game, and it plays in two distinct phases so I can teach each phase as it comes"), Dixit ("Beautiful presentation and fun"), and Spyfall 2 ("It plays up to twelve and it's easy for everyone to stay engaged").

John R. Ilko's basement walls are lined with shelves filled with games, many of which are still in their original shrink-wrap. ("That may well be a sickness in itself," he jokes.) When you play at John's house, the chosen game is likely to be one that nobody at the table has ever played before. "Very often, our games are 'learning' games," John says. "If someone makes a play that is clearly not in their best interest, depending on the situation and the individual, I might gently and pleasantly suggest that they perhaps have a stronger play available."

The language John uses to describe the situation—you can practically hear his shoes tapping the top of the eggshells he's walking on—is indicative of how sensitive that decision can sometimes be. It's a fine line. Are you offering a helping hand or coming across as bossy? Are you providing strategy tips or implying that someone is Not Very Good at Gaming? John's approach is the right one, and he recognizes that when people learn a game for the first time it's easy to forget or misunderstand a rule or lose track of the ways to score points.

The first time I played Ticket to Ride, a game with relatively simple rules, I forgot that the value of any unfinished destination tickets in your hand at the end of the game is subtracted from your score. As a result, I finished with negative points. A *lot* of negative points. I enjoyed that particular game anyway and have played Ticket to Ride at least a hundred times since, but I sure wouldn't have been upset if someone had reminded me of that rule when they saw me drawing so many destination tickets.

Everyone at the table, John says, should "have a sense that fairness and fun are the main themes of the evening." When a new game is being taught, particularly to a relatively new gamer, John goes so far as to allow players to take back a poor play. That's smart, because if a new player knows they've made a bad play, they can grow frustrated and feel like their position in the game is hopeless. That's never enjoyable.

One sometimes underappreciated element of introducing non-gamers to new games is the quality of the game's components. In her contribution to the book *Rerolling Boardgames: Essays on Themes, Systems, Experiences and Ideologies*, Melissa Rogerson, PhD, a board game researcher from Melbourne, Australia, discusses how central the physical components are to the enjoyment of a board game: "They represent the game's theme, but they are more than empty theming; they look and feel beautiful, but they are more than simple ornaments; they enable and invite play, but they are more than merely toys; they represent information, but they are not purely a data storage or calculation tool."[1]

For example, when game publisher Days of Wonder burst onto the scene in the mid-2000s one of the first things people noticed was how fantastic the components in their games were. I already mentioned Ticket to Ride, but the three-dimensional palace in Cleopatra and the

Society of Architects and the 144 detailed plastic miniatures in Memoir '44 likewise grabbed players' attention before they ever sat down at the table.

High-quality components give players the sense that the game itself is high quality—and the impact is measurable. A study conducted by Nils Jostmann, PhD, of the University of Amsterdam concluded that "much as weight makes people invest more physical effort in dealing with concrete objects, it also makes people invest more cognitive effort in dealing with abstract issues."[2] In the study, participants were asked to guess the conversion rate of various currencies. Some were given a clipboard weighing 1.5 pounds; the others were given a clipboard weighing 2.3 pounds. The foreign currencies were assigned a higher value by those with the heavier clipboards. Other tests not involving money confirmed the results.

In terms of games, I believe our tendency to assign more importance to heavier items manifests itself in several ways. Most obviously, games with deep strategic possibilities are described as "heavy" games. Even gamers who don't enjoy playing those games tend to respect them. "Light" games, on the other hand, are more easily dismissed as "fillers" and "fluff." But quality components can overcome that. Dixit, a light party game, includes eighty-four cards, six wooden rabbits, a couple dozen cardboard markers, and a scoring track. On the surface, there's not much there. But the first time someone sees Dixit, they're bound to be captivated by the imaginative art on the cards, the way the scoring track is nestled inside the game box, and the cuteness of those rabbits. A great deal of care was obviously put into every element of Dixit. Without that, it would have come and gone in a flash. Instead, it has won multiple gaming awards and sold millions of copies of the base game and its numerous expansions.

Other games that garner attention for their visual presentation are Takenoko (with colorful plastic bamboo trees), Parks (featuring dramatic art from the Fifty-Nine Parks Print Series), and the War of the Ring Collector's Edition (which comes in a huge wooden box designed to look like an Elven book). Games that make great use of all three dimensions also win oohs and aahs, including Fireball Island: The Curse of Vul-Kar (volcanic explosions cause mayhem all across the board), Rhino Hero (players build a tower that can reach several feet tall), and Niagara (the edge of the game box serves as the waterfall).

Qwirkle, the amazing abstract game designed by Susan McKinley Ross, is a great example of making a game instantly appealing. It consists of 108 wooden blocks painted with six shapes in six colors (so there are three of each block in the game). The black background makes the vibrant colors—blue, green, red, yellow, purple, and orange—stand out from across the room. Of course, even the best presentation won't save a bad game. The look and feel of Qwirkle helps, to be sure, but the main reason that people have bought more than four million copies is that it's downright fun to play.

Certain gaming accessories can also cause people to take notice. For example, as a hobbyist woodworker, I've built several dice towers. I enjoy games with dice, and the sound of the dice rolling across the table is good. But the sound of dice clattering down a well-constructed dice tower is awesome. The entire process lasts only a second or two, but by the time the dice shoot out the bottom of the tower, the anticipation has grown so much that often everyone at the table is leaning over to get a look at the roll.

Needless to say, this cuts both ways. Bad components and unappealing art can turn people off. As Dr. Rogerson says, "Some players actively avoid games if they don't like the art style, even if they find the game itself interesting."[3]

TREATING GAMES WITH
CARE AND RESPECT

We talked in the last chapter about game-friendly food and drink and making sure that your games don't wind up as collectors of powdered cheese, but a far more dangerous force looms, waiting to wreak havoc and bring destruction: your friends.

One afternoon several years ago, I was playing games at Anthony Rubbo's house. Anthony, the designer of games like Dark Seas, Clash of Vikings, and the delightful (and underrated) partnership card game Hey Waiter!, had invited about a dozen people over for a weekend of gaming and we were split into three tables. My group played Concept, a party game in which one player tries to get the others to guess a word (such as *angel*) by placing markers on various icons (such as a mannequin head and an open circle). I set the empty box on the floor next to my chair and promptly forgot about it. When I stood up to get something from the kitchen, I stepped right on the box. Predictably, my foot fared much better than the box, which was flattened. I was mortified, but Anthony was very understanding. I bought him a new copy right away—which is the appropriate response when you destroy someone's game—and I'm pretty sure he'll invite me back. Someday.

Years before my Godzilla impression at Anthony's house, Beth and I visited our friends Warren and Sharon Madden (Sharon is also director of the Dice Tower East game convention). We played A la Carte, Karl-Heinz Schmiel's game of culinary wackiness. One of the things you're required to do during A la Carte is shake a dispenser that contains small, irregularly shaped pieces representing various spices. Typically, somewhere between zero and four spice pieces come out. When I shook it, a piece of spice popped out of the bottle, bounced once on the table, and then—after floating through space and time in a graceful slow-motion arc—landed directly in an air vent on the floor. "We never found the piece," Sharon says. (Not for lack of trying, I might add!) "And while we don't live in that house any longer, for all we know, it's still somewhere in the duct!"

(A quick aside: whoever decided to put air vents in floors was not a gamer. I'm not the only one with a horror story. Mike Young, who meets friends for board games every week, was playing Orleans when a wooden worker piece rolled off the table. Predictably, it found its way into a nearby vent. "We spent half an hour working out how to get it back," Mike says. "This included sticking a camera down the vent into the duct to see where the piece was and using a vacuum cleaner to retrieve it.")

I tell these stories not to dissuade you from inviting me to your home to play games, although that would be a perfectly reasonable reaction. Rather, I want to emphasize the idea that even when people try to take care of your games, accidents happen. A lot. When they do, it's time to take a deep breath and remind yourself that you love your friend, that all material goods are ephemeral—whatever it takes to make sure you don't lose your temper, throw the guest out of your house, and declare an end to all game nights forevermore.

Not all destruction is accidental. We've all heard stories about people responding to danger with adrenaline-fueled feats of strength they could never accomplish otherwise. Dan Hoffman has seen rage at the game table lead to a similar outcome. "I was playing Castle of Magic with Scott Buckwalter," he says. "It's a game where you roll tons of dice, and rolling a six is an instant fail. Scott's famous for rolling exactly what he doesn't need. After his zillionth six in a row, he took the die and threw it. When it hit the floor, the die shattered. I'd never seen that before. Somewhere in my office I still have the remains."

If you've never had the privilege of setting up a 1970s war game, the process involves dozens or hundreds, or even thousands, of small cardboard counters and a tweezer-like tool to place them in the proper location.

In at least one case, those cardboard pieces provided a convenient way for a player to express strong emotions. "My uncle-in-law was playing The Longest Day," says Michael Holmquist. (That game has 2,603 cardboard counters.) "After getting attacked and decimated by the other players, he dumped all of the counters into the middle of the board, poured his soda on top, then made a mixture of cardboard and soda with his hands." I like to imagine that Michael's uncle-in-law cackled like Emperor Palpatine while he did this, but the truth is not so dramatic. "Immediately after he was done making his mush, he took his still-in-shrink copy and gave it to the game owner," Michael says.

If something like this happens at one of your game nights, be sure to take a moment so your response doesn't escalate the situation. It's quite likely that the issue is something more than the game itself. This might be a good time to take a break from gaming, to let people have some space to calm down, and to check in with the offending guest.

PETS LOVE GAMES, BUT DO GAMES LOVE PETS?

Humans aren't the only source of damage to games. At our previous house, most of our games were stored on open shelves in the basement, where our cats liked to hang out. The 1999 Avalon Hill edition of Sid Sackson's Acquire, which was sold in a large box with plastic components and remains the best-produced edition of the classic game, was stored on a lower shelf.

One of our cats, however, did not appreciate the greatness of Acquire—and certainly not the reasons that particular edition stands out. What he did appreciate was the fact that his claws could easily dig into the box. By the time he was done, it looked like one end of the game box had been on the wrong side of an Edward Scissorhands tantrum.

Brian Stormont remembers playing Freedom in the Galaxy: The Star Rebellions, 5764 AD with a high school friend. (Published in 1979 by Avalon Hill, Freedom in the Galaxy was rather obviously inspired by the first *Star Wars* movie.) The game included four hundred cardboard counters, which Brian and his friend kept in the open box cover. "My friend's cat thought it made a nice litter box," Brian says. "As much as he tried, there was no way to get rid of the smell of cat urine." Years later, Brian bought him a used copy of the game, which had been long out of print, as a birthday present.

Before I continue sharing examples, I'd like to emphasize how much I love cats. At one time, Beth and I had five. They were phenomenal pets and we have amazing memories of all of them. Nonetheless, there is a body of anecdotal evidence that strongly suggests cats and games don't always get along.

Brad Minnigh recalls playing a game of Battle Masters on the floor. (You need an extraordinarily large table on which to play Battle Masters—otherwise it's the floor. Milton Bradley's philosophy in 1992 seemed to be "bigger is better" as the vinyl mat that serves as a game board is fifty-five inches wide by fifty-seven inches long—more than twenty square feet.) "My cat went crazy and dove under the map," Brad says. "The armies flew everywhere. Several spears were broken, but it was hilarious."

Dominion is the game of choice for cat owner Mary Anne Miller Rodrigues and her husband, who play it nearly every night. Although she tries to keep their cat off the dining room table, it doesn't always observe the rules. One day, she was clearing the table to wash the tablecloth and discovered a surprise. "I picked up the stack of moats (a card type in Dominion)," she says. "They were wet on the top and mostly stuck together straight to the bottom of the pile. The cat had chosen our moats as the place to cough up her watery hairball. Gross!" Mary Anne's efforts to clean and dry the cards kind of worked, but she replaced them with a nicer deck she bought online.

Cats aren't the only animals capable of surprising their owners. Jim McMahon remembers playing Kingdom Builder at his friend Mike's house. "His corgi was wearing a 'cone of shame' and hanging out by the table," Jim says. "Mike dropped one of his wooden houses on the floor. The dog used the cone to scoop it up and swallowed it. The best part is Mike followed that dog outside for days with a baggie. He finally recovered the house, which was swallowed whole without any bite marks. The moral of this story is: if you ever play Mike's copy of Kingdom Builder, do not choose black as your color."

Rachel Gay says her schnoodle, Calliope, "had a taste for fine things when she was a puppy." Two LPs by French pianist Jacque Loussier and an iPhone serve as irrefutable evidence. "Calliope never went near my games," Rachel says, "until I opened my copy of Tammany Hall. I came home a few days after to find two of the box corners nibbled through. Only that game, though." Unfortunately, Calliope can't speak so we may never know if she opposes political corruption . . . or has a taste for it.

If you have pets, you probably have a similar story or two. While there's humor to be found in those situations, remember that game components may look like yummy snacks to our furry friends— especially the small wooden pieces, which are serious choking hazards. Be sure to keep your meeples somewhere your pets can't get to them.

SEMI-COOPERATIVE GAMES

Semi-cooperative games—those featuring one or more hidden enemies or traitors—are a special delight to me. The genre tends to be polarizing, but those who enjoy semi-coops tend to relish not knowing if the person sitting next to them is on their team. Others detest the tension that uncertainty brings. In part, the starkly differing opinions emerge from the fact that the traitor is, by the very nature of being a traitor, required to lie to the other players. The traitor must convince everyone else, for as long as possible, that they want the team to win. Under that pressure, some players can't help but giggle, or stammer, or send some other unconscious signal that they're not part of the team.

Perhaps the best-known semi-coop is Werewolf, which is played by some groups as Mafia. It's a good example because in this game, everyone knows there are two sides: the villagers and the werewolves. But only the werewolves know who's who. The entire game consists of a series of night phases, during which the werewolves collaborate to eliminate a villager from the game, and day phases, during which the villagers try to agree that one player is a werewolf and thus needs to be dispatched. During each day phase, everyone—villagers and werewolves alike—participates in the debate. The discussions can be intense as people study body language and analyze every comment, looking for any hint that might give away someone's identity. After a few minutes, the moderator calls for a vote and everyone simultaneously points to the person they're prepared to eliminate from the game. That person reveals their identity. If they were a werewolf, the villagers rejoice for being that much closer to a victory. But if they were a villager, the disappointment is palpable.

Semi-coops are imbued with paranoia. *I know Bill's on my side*, you may think. *I'm pretty sure, at least. Wait. If Bill's on my side, why did he make that move?* More than once after my wife and I were involved in a semi-coop game, she's punched me playfully and said "I can't believe I trusted you again." I'm pretty sure what she means is "I'm impressed with how well you played that game."

The first semi-coop I experienced was Shadows over Camelot, designed by Bruno Cathala and Serge Laget and set in the world of King Arthur. At the start of the game, eight loyalty cards are shuffled and one is dealt to each player (the game is for three to seven players). Of the eight cards, one is a traitor card. If that card is dealt to a player, it gives them a secret objective: make sure the team (i.e., everyone else) loses. The card distribution gives Shadows over Camelot a wonderful twist: it's never certain that there actually is a traitor. In a four-player game, the odds are fifty-fifty. Even in a seven-player game, there's a 12.5 percent chance that there's no traitor. But the mere possibility of a traitor changes behavior remarkably. Every move is scrutinized for evidence of a turncoat.

Battlestar Galactica may be the semi-coop where the theme blends most perfectly with the game system. There might not be any cylons (traitors) for the first part of the game, but there will always be at least one before the game ends. Based on the 2004 to 2009 Syfy television series of the same name (a reboot of the original ABC series that aired for a single season in 1978 and 1979), Battlestar Galactica sees the human players trying to move a fleet of spaceships a certain distance. The cylon player(s) must prevent them from doing so. During the game, accusations will fly and there are moments where no one knows who can be trusted. From time to time, suspected cylons will be thrown into the brig.

Another favorite is The Resistance, where players are secretly sorted into teams of Resistance operatives and Imperial spies. As with other semi-coop games, one issue to watch for is a player who gets too invested. Some players will not stop accusing an opponent of, for example, being an Imperial spy because they can't understand why everyone else doesn't see what they see. On the flip side, some players aren't built to lie—or to weather constant accusations that they're lying. Using a timer to limit the length of each round is a simple way to counteract those situations.

Other semi-coop games include Deception: Murder in Hong Kong, in which one of the police detectives investigating a murder is actually the killer, and Dead of Winter, a zombie-themed game where players have a common victory condition—but they also have individual secret objectives, making it possible that everyone wins, everyone loses, or some players win and the others lose. My favorite semi-coop by far is Betrayal at House on the Hill (see my review of Betrayal Legacy in chapter 7). One reason it stands out from the others is that the traitor, revealed to everyone partway through the game, isn't hidden at all. The tension in Betrayal is created by the fact that the traitor and the rest of the players, who work as a team, have different victory conditions—and neither knows exactly what the other is trying to accomplish.

THE FLOW OF A GAME NIGHT

Great movies have an opening that draws you in, a middle that leaves you awed or surprised, and an end that satisfies. It's much the same with a great meal: appetizer, main course, dessert. Do you see where I'm going with this? Great game nights are no different. Don't get me wrong: if there's only time for a quick round of Blokus or everyone wants to dive right into a two-hour strategy game like Terraforming Mars, I'm all in. But for me, the best game nights have a flow. I love it when things work out so there's a quick opener followed by a strategy game or two and a closer that lets the brain begin to relax.

Particularly when your game-night crowd is too big to play a single game together, that kind of flow is key. As a bonus, starting with a short opener or two gives stragglers time to arrive without fearing that they'll be on the sidelines for an hour while everyone else finishes their games.

For example, if game night starts at 6:30 p.m. and you have seven players on hand at the appointed hour, it would be tempting to go ahead and split into a group of three and a group of four. Maybe one group starts Gloomhaven while the other launches Gaia Project. But both games take one to two hours, and if another player shows up fifteen minutes in (maybe they got stuck in traffic, or had to work late, or . . . you get the idea), they have to sit on the sidelines for at least forty-five minutes watching everyone else have fun. You can either hope you have enough chips on hand, or you can invite your group to open with a game like Incan Gold (three to eight players, thirty minutes or less) and the latecomer won't have to wait long at all.

Barry "BJ" Rozas, host of the YouTube channel Board Game Gumbo, agrees with that approach. "Tempo the night like a meal," he says. "Start with a quick fifteen-to-twenty-minute card game that's easy for people to watch or join in." He recommends No Thanks! and Silver, two great options. "Have a meaty game for the middle, even if the definition of meaty is light considering the experience of the expected attendees. Finish it up with a nice, fun party game that has everyone laughing."

Now, if you're attending a game night and something happens to cause you to be late, you bear some responsibility for letting the host know, if you can. If you show up unannounced forty-five minutes into game night and everyone's already involved in games, you have only yourself to blame.

As the host, it's perfectly appropriate to set specific start times. Longer games, like the three- or four-hour epic *Star Wars*: Rebellion, often get scheduled in advance so everyone knows who's playing and when they need to arrive. Jared Vento occasionally organizes events that are completely devoted to longer games.

As game night winds down, some players will keep suggesting more games. You may be one of those players. (I am!) But you're the

Great Games for Large Groups

DECEPTION: MURDER IN HONG KONG

Four to twelve players
Designed by Tobey Ho
Published by Iello (2014)

There's been a murder in Hong Kong . . . and you're a suspect. In Deception: Murder in Hong Kong, a team of detectives must take vague clues provided by a somewhat evasive forensic scientist and determine who did it and how. Or, if you're the killer, you're on your own and must try to deceive your fellow detectives.

Each player, other than the forensic scientist, is given an equal number of means cards (e.g., brick and pistol) and clue cards (e.g., computer and map), all of which are placed faceup. The scientist hints at which combination of cards is correct. The simple design underscores a fantastic system. When cards are as different as knife and rope but as similar as pills and poison, the players must create a story behind the clues to convince one another which two cards are the right answer. All of this while the killer tries to throw them off the scent.

Everyone's limited to a single guess at the solution; because of this, the tension is high. Still, no player is ever out of the game—even those who make incorrect accusations can participate in the group deliberations. But in Deception: Murder in Hong Kong the motive behind the stories being spun is as much a mystery as the crime you're striving to solve.

DIXIT: ODYSSEY

Three to twelve players
Designed by Jean-Louis Roubira
Published by Libellud (2011)

Once in a very great while, a game comes along that feels like it should have always existed. The rules are so simple and the play so engaging you quickly know it's a classic. This is one of those games.

In Dixit: Odyssey, players start with a hand of six cards, each with a beautiful illustration of a unique fanciful scene. You might see a blacksmith forging hearts, a robotic octopus holding a lantern, or a magnifying glass revealing houses in a footprint. An initial storyteller selects one card from their hand and comes up with a clue they hope will get most players, but not all of them, to guess it. Everyone else then examines their hand to find a competing card, something that will lead the other players to choose their card instead. These cards are shuffled together and dealt out faceup. The players then vote on which card they believe is the storyteller's. Points are earned for guessing the correct card and for other players guessing your card. The storyteller earns points only if at least one player, but not all, guessed their card.

This obvious-but-not-too-obvious mechanism creates wonderful gaming moments as players connect over surprising shared experiences and references. Other Dixit games are available, but Odyssey plays with up to twelve, so it's great for larger groups. There are also a variety of expansions that add more gorgeous cards into the mix.

INCAN GOLD

Three to eight players
Designed by Bruno Faidutti and Alan R. Moon
Published by Eagle-Gryphon Games (2005)

Incan Gold has a number of appealing qualities: it handles higher player counts well, it's easy to teach, and it has the betcha-can't-eat-just-one feeling that often finds players wanting to play again imme-diately after finishing the first game. The game is a short five rounds, often lasting fifteen to twenty minutes.

It's also one of the purest distillations of the press-your-luck genre of games. Players descend into a jewel-filled temple and after each card flip must simultaneously decide whether they will stay inside (hop-ing to find more treasure) or run for the exit and be satisfied with what they've gathered so far (instead of risking a horrible fate).

The decision is complicated by the need to amass more treasure than any other player, the reward for leaving by yourself (some treasure is left on the path to be scooped up by exiting players), and the ever-increasing chance of bad things happening. The deck includes five types of calamities, and when a second card of the same type appears—for example, a second snake—every player still in the cave loses all the jewels they've picked up and the round is over.

Simultaneously deciding whether to drop out is a nail-biting, do-you-feel-lucky? moment and a key part of what makes Incan Gold so enjoyable. The European version of the game is known as Diamant (with players descending into a cave rather than a temple). Either ver-sion is well worth your time and gaming dollars.

ONE NIGHT ULTIMATE WEREWOLF

Three to ten players
Designed by Ted Alspach and Akihisa Okui
Published by Bézier Games (2014)

One Night Ultimate Werewolf—a quick-playing version of Were-wolf—is a ten-minute, app-narrated party game of hidden identities that is sure to lead to laugh-out-loud accusations at your game night.

Each player receives a secret role at the start of the game. Some are villagers; others are werewolves. Most also have a special power to either help their team or cause general mischief. The Seer, for example, can peek at another player's card; the Troublemaker blindly switches the cards of two other players. After looking at their roles, players close their eyes as the app narrates a night phase. When the app calls a role, that player can wake up (open their eyes) to use their special power. Also during the night phase, the werewolves learn each other's identities, an element of gameplay that allows them to cover each other's tracks.

When day breaks and everyone wakes up, players have a few minutes to deduce the identity of a werewolf. Accusations, denials, trickery, and cover-ups abound. When the app's timer runs out, the players vote, and if a werewolf is caught, the villager team prevails. But if a villager is nabbed instead, the werewolves win.

The artwork on the cards is fun, and the app ensures that gameplay goes smoothly every time. But the best part of One Night Ultimate Werewolf may be the way you can mix the roles—and thus different powers—into each game, creating seemingly endless combinations of werewolf-themed conspiracies.

SUSHI GO PARTY!

Two to eight players
Designed by Phil Walker-Harding
Published by Gamewright (2016)

Whether you like sushi or not, Sushi Go Party! is a splendid card-drafting game where you try to build the best meal out of a variety of menu options like sashimi and temaki, and don't forget pudding for dessert!

Much like 7 Wonders, players are dealt a hand of cards, then simultaneously choose a card and pass the remainder of the hand to the next player. Cards score in various ways, all clearly marked on the cards themselves. For example, the majority of cards score only in the round they are played—but dessert cards are saved and scored at the end of the final round.

The game comes with more than twenty card sets, eight of which are chosen for each game. The board includes a scoring track as well as recessed spaces to hold the scoring rules for the cards being used in that game.

Bright colorful artwork (with a bit of whimsy) and straightforward rules make Sushi Go Party! a great light strategy game to open the evening or wrap it up.

MORE GREAT GAMES FOR LARGE GROUPS

CODENAMES
two to eight players, designed by Vlaada Chvátil,
published by Czech Games Edition, 2015

DECRYPTO
three to eight players, designed by Thomas Dagenais-Lespérance,
published by Iello, 2018

THE RESISTANCE
five to ten players, designed by Don Eskridge,
published by Indie Boards & Cards, 2009

SABOTEUR
three to ten players, designed by Fréderic Moyersoen,
published by Amigo, 2004

TIME'S UP!
four to twelve players, designed by Peter Sarrett,
published by R&R Games, 1999

5

Extra Large Group Game Nights
—eleven to twenty players—

The first challenge of a game night with eleven or more players is finding the right place to hold it. Unless your home is pretty spacious, you'll need somewhere else to gather. If you do host in your home, guests will likely be gaming in multiple rooms—perhaps on multiple floors.

Once you work out the logistics, a game night of this size can be remarkably fun. There's no shortage of players so chances are good that multiple games are being played at all times, giving everyone the opportunity to play a game they enjoy with players they like. If you're able to end the night with a large group game like Catch Phrase or Werewolf, so much the better.

TABLES AND CHAIRS
(AND OTHER FURNITURE)

I mentioned our friends Tom and Dana earlier; although it doesn't happen enough, Beth and I love visiting them for game nights. Tom and Dana are great, of course, but they also own a dining room table that's perfect for games. It may be magical, because it's nothing but a large square and yet somehow manages to be comfortable for anywhere from four to eight players. When Tom told me one day that their house had caught fire, my very first question was about the table: Is it okay? (You may be thinking: *Really? That was your first question?* In my defense, I assumed he would've said so if Dana or their children had been hurt in any way.) Luckily, the fire—caused by questionable storage of refuse from a corn furnace—only did superficial damage to the table.

Tom and Dana have taken that table with them from Carlisle, Pennsylvania; to Pittsburgh; then to Columbus, Ohio; and most recently the Jersey shore. Tom was one of my college roommates. We've been friends for three decades. But if he ever gets rid of that table, our relationship will be on the rocks.

If you already have a great game table, outstanding! A good table will have plenty of space for the game board along with player-specific components, such as Zombicide's survivor identity cards, and shared components, like Zombicide's many cards, tokens, and zombie miniatures. The size of the table you need is vastly different for a massive game like Eldritch Horror than for a modestly sized game like Codenames. But size is not the only consideration, and playing on a table that's too large can be just as frustrating as one that's too small.

I love massive game tables, small game tables, game tables with cup holders and drawers, game tables with sunken surfaces, game tables of all types. But when it comes right down to it, any flat surface can be a game table. For example, my friend Delene Lantz bought an old trunk and painted a checkerboard on the top. The surface can be used to play games, which are then stored inside the trunk itself. Perfect!

You don't need a table that's dedicated to gaming, of course. Gamers around the world, including Beth and me, do just fine on a kitchen or dining room table, and there's a long-loved tradition of spreading out on the floor—if your joints allow you to. Whatever table you use (if you use one at all—games like Time's Up! and Werewolf don't need a table), remember to focus on the comfort of your guests. Playing backgammon on a coffee table while sitting on the floor isn't something older gamers are likely to appreciate, and even the spryest among us would be hard-pressed to tolerate a lengthier game with such a setup. (If you have no alternative to seating your guests on the floor, provide plenty of pillows. Large, soft pillows.)

If you don't yet have a game table and are ready to make the investment, there are many choices, including numerous companies that manufacture high-quality tables designed especially for gaming.

Wyrmwood is one such manufacturer. The Taunton, Massachusetts, company offers two main styles of table: the Sojourn, which seats four to eight, and the Prophecy, which seats six to ten. Each is available in a variety of woods, including black walnut, zebrawood, and spalted maple. You can add options like a lift mechanism to raise and lower the playing surface and a spill-resistant wooden dining topper that can be placed over the fabric game surface for meals. Other manufacturers of top-end game tables include Bandpass Design, Game On Tables, Geeknson, Hammered Game Tables, and Rathskellers. With a little searching, you can find even more.

But high quality comes with a corresponding price tag. For most tables from those companies, you're likely to spend well over $1,000. For some of the largest, most tricked-out tables, you may (believe it or not) cross the $10,000 threshold. If you want to spend the money, more power to you. But getting a game table doesn't have to be an expensive proposition.

I made a table that seats up to six players out of three-quarter-inch plywood using only a jigsaw, a drill with a hole saw attached, a pair of folding legs, a screwdriver, and some screws. I installed six cup holders (that's what the hole saw was for, although the cup holders are purely optional), and the table works like a charm. It's not fancy, but it's functional. It took me less than a day to complete it, including protecting the top with two coats of polyurethane. The finished product is thirty-two inches wide by sixty inches long, rounded on both ends, and the supplies only cost about a hundred dollars.

If you'd like to build your own table but want something a little more substantial, find "DIY Gaming Table for $150" on YouTube. More than 3.3 million people have watched Gaminggeek build what is, for most of us, a dream table using fairly basic tools and lumber. He graciously made the plans available for free, and he posted two follow-up videos detailing the five things he loves most about the table and five ways it could be improved. To sample other ideas before starting your own table, browse the thread "Game Table Design Series: Completed BGG Game Tables" at BoardGameGeek's "Do It Yourself" forum, where BGGers show off their own homemade game tables.

Another affordable option is a simple card table, which seats four players, measures roughly three feet by three feet, and has foldable legs for easy storage. Good card tables are available for about fifty dollars, with sturdier versions selling for about a hundred dollars. When I was growing up, my parents regularly played the card game bridge with their friends. When it was their turn to host, they set up two card tables and eight folding chairs in our living room. The dining room table was the snack station, always full of foods seemingly chosen specifically because I didn't like them.

With a little searching and some luck, you might even be able to get a great table for free. When he was a pastor, Mark Jackson acquired a massive table rejected from his church's fellowship hall because, as he says, "it weighed a ton, so no one wanted to manhandle it around the room." He loved that four-foot by eight-foot table in large part because it was "perfect for giant Heroscape battles."

The table may be the most visible piece of furniture in your game room, but it's far from alone. Comfortable chairs and good lighting shouldn't be overlooked. Ideally, chairs will have padded seats and solid construction suitable for various body types. Some people prefer chairs with arms, but larger gamers are often more comfortable in chairs without.

One lesson that most of us learn at some point, occasionally the hard way, is that you should never lean back in a chair. In middle school, my math teacher Mr. Beck made this point clear. Any time he caught a student leaning back in a chair, that student had to stand and hold the chair for the rest of the class period. I may very well own the school record in time spent holding a chair. (Perhaps unsurprisingly, Mr. Beck was also the woodshop teacher.)

To this day, Mr. Beck remains one of my favorite teachers. However, his lesson failed to get through my thick skull. One night a few years ago, Beth and I were visiting Christine Biancheria and Sue Frietsche on a Saturday night. While sitting in a very nice chair that matched their very nice game table, I leaned back. I'm not a small man so the physics of the situation did not favor the chair. It broke. I fell to the floor, uninjured but with an immediate recognition of what had to be done. Christine was out picking up our dinner order, so clearly the chair had to be hidden so that I could order a new one and have it replaced before she realized anything was amiss.

Sadly, my plan never came to fruition. Christine arrived with the food, the jig was up, and by the time I called the company on Monday to order a replacement, the nice man who answered told me that Christine had beaten me to the punch. I tried to convince him to let me pay for it, but he was (wisely) unwilling to step into a dispute between friends. (I later made a contribution to one of Christine's favorite charities, so my conscience is clean. Mostly. I still feel like I owe Mr. Beck an apology.)

I take some solace in the fact that I'm far from the only person to experience a game-related furniture disaster.

Wei-Hwa Huang, an internationally recognized puzzler and codesigner of the game Roll for the Galaxy, was visiting Dominion designer Donald X. Vaccarino for a playtest session with Tom Lehmann, designer of Race for the Galaxy and codesigner of Roll for the Galaxy. "We playtested a few games, including ones that would later become Kingdom Builder and Nefarious," Wei-Hwa says. "I got up to get a drink, and when I sat down the next time I heard a crack and found myself sitting on the floor, holding half of a chair in each hand by the chair arms. The seat had split cleanly in half."

When she visited a local gaming club, all June King wanted to do was play her new, still-in-shrink copy of Reiner Knizia's game Taj Mahal. "I set my bag of games next to my chair and sat down," she says. "The chair was old and the legs were welded on. I leaned over to pull a game out of my bag and a rusty weld separated. The chair canted, dumping me on my bag. My knee went right into the Taj Mahal box, crushing the corner like a pancake." (I tip my hat to June for her use of *canted*, a wonderful word dating back to the sixteenth century.)

Tables and chairs aren't the only items of furniture that affect game night. When Rob Simons and his wife went shopping for a chandelier, he had one specific requirement. "I was very insistent on getting an upward-facing light that would bounce off the ceiling rather than a downward-facing light," he says. "This was to help prevent glare on glossy cards."

The older I get, the more essential bright, non-glaring lights are to my enjoyment of a gaming session. Some graphic designers are absolute geniuses when it comes to making the board and all of the text on cards readable in less-than-ideal lighting conditions, but others have failed to grasp the concept and insist on putting gray text on a slightly darker gray background or some likewise terrible combination. So I applaud Rob's dedication to good game-room lighting.

If you're not in the market for a new chandelier, consider adding one or two upward-facing floor lamps to your game room. In terms of bulb type, the only rule is to avoid fluorescent lights, which over time can increase fatigue. LED bulbs can be purchased in various color temperatures. Lower temperatures (2200K to 2700K) tend to give off an amber or yellowish hue and are more suitable for rooms where relaxation is the focus. Higher temperatures (3000K, bright white; 4000K, cool white; or 5000K, daylight) tend to be best for game rooms, but within that range the choice comes down to personal preference. Dimmers can help you dial in the exact right amount of light.

HOW TO STORE YOUR GAMES

At first blush, how and where you store your games may not seem directly related to your duties as a game-night host, but it will have a big impact on what gets played.

Many gamers, myself included, swear by the Kallax shelves available at Ikea. Their size (the interior of each cube is a little more than thirteen inches wide by thirteen inches tall by fifteen inches deep) is perfect for holding most games published today in a way that makes them easy to scan. The old proverb "Out of sight, out of mind" applies to games, too. If some or most of your games are hidden away, they're far less likely to get pulled out on game night.

Randy Cox's organization system lends credence to that point. He keeps about half a dozen games (the ones "that get played") on a former aquarium base in the dining room. "Another twenty or so are there because they were played in the past year," he says. The rest of his nine-hundred-plus games are stored in his junk room.

Every gamer has their own way of organizing their collection. Some focus on box size, keeping games of similar sizes together with perhaps some exceptions for games from the same family, such as Catan, Pandemic, or Ticket to Ride. That's a practical approach since it will help maximize the number of games you can fit in your space. Others sort their games first by the number of players—keeping all of their two-player games close together, for example—and within those groups by complexity and how long it takes to play. Some treat their game collection like a library, arranging them by the designer's last name. Mine are organized, at least loosely, by theme. All the deduction games are together, for example, as are the race games, the dexterity games, and the party games.

Some, like Rodney Somerstein and Rik Van Horn, look for space wherever it can be found. "Mine tend to be organized by, 'Oh look, a square inch of space without a game'," Rodney says. "Or, 'That stack of games isn't too tall yet.' Most rooms of my house have at least one game. Many have quite a few more." Rik also has games in every room of his house—and in his car. "Some on shelves," he says, "some on tables, dressers, hutches, or anywhere there's an open space."

Ross Connell, a freelance photographer in Nottingham, UK, organizes his games based on box color, creating a look that shifts from white on the left shelves through red, green, and blue until reaching black on the rightmost shelves. "Large game collections can dominate small spaces, but they can also be an opportunity to add more character to a room," he says. "I bought these shelves specifically to make my collection, and by blending from lighter tones in the middle of the space through to the dark boxes toward the corner it feels more like a feature of the room than a collection occupying space."

Sometimes, organization exists more on a wish list than it does in reality. "I try to keep similar weight games together, but it's gone off the rails," says Leslie Cheung. "We have a cabinet shelf for small and lightweight games. I tried grouping deck-builders on a shelf in the den and older games on another shelf, but everything else is completely random in multiple areas."

Some games are so sprawling or have so many expansions they practically require you to come up with creative storage solutions. My hundreds of Heroscape figures are housed in plastic cases built by hardware manufacturer Stanley to hold small tools and parts. In some cases, game publishers offer their own storage products. In 2020, Stronghold Games ran a wildly successful Kickstarter for Terraforming Mars: Big Box, which includes nearly one hundred three-dimensional terrain tiles in a box big enough to store the base game plus five expansions. The Broken Token, an independent company, has worked with publishers to create wonderful wooden box inserts and other high-quality organizers for games like Gloomhaven, King of Tokyo, and Wingspan.

Whatever shelving and organization systems you use, bear in mind that games kept in the basement need to be protected from flooding and other common basement issues like pests, mold, and humidity. Our current house, thankfully, has a dry basement and we keep our games in the finished portion. But our previous basement would occasionally take on water during heavy storms. To avoid water damage, I used strips of treated lumber to raise the shelves.

TRASH TALK AND TABLE TALK

Trash talk and table talk are two very different things, but both can have a dramatic impact on the enjoyment of a game night unless the players are on the same page.

When I play games with certain friends, good-natured trash talk—along the lines of "Really? You think that's a good move?"—is an expected part of the experience. In some cases, if they didn't hurl some trash talk my way during a game I'd wonder what I had done to offend them. But that's not true in most of the games I play, and it's important to recognize the difference.

To players who don't like trash talk, it can come across as obnoxious and demeaning. In my experience, groups tend to self-police trash talk quickly and it doesn't develop into a serious issue. But some people don't understand, or don't care about, the impact their trash talk is having on others. That's something the host needs to keep an ear out for.

Table talk is an entirely different creature. Merriam-Webster's definition of *table talk* ("informal conversation at or as if at a dining table") does not (yet) reference tabletop games. Wikipedia, on the other hand, has an entry all about game-related table talk, which it defines as "In certain card games . . . communication by a player with another player about the cards in their hand, usually contrary to the rules of the game. Such communication may be through explicitly naming cards, but it is far more common to try to give hints which the opposing players will think innocent, but which will be understood by the player's partner." Urban Dictionary's definition is similar to Wikipedia's, and they're both spot-on—except that table talk is not limited to card games.

In practice, table talk can range from sharing information with a teammate in team games to encouraging other players to make moves that will disadvantage a certain person, often the perceived leader. Unless you're playing with a group of good friends who have developed an understanding about what level of table talk is acceptable, it should generally be avoided.

Note that table talk is nothing like the kind of rules assistance discussed in chapter 4. When you're introducing a new game, some helpful pointers can be well received. Table talk, on the other hand, is by its nature intended to create an advantage for the person making the comments or to disadvantage one or more opponents.

Consider a hypothetical three-player game of Ticket to Ride. Let's say Gloria needs to claim a three-train route with blue cards to complete a lengthy connection. Harry goes next, adding two cards to his hand. Before Susan takes her turn, Harry says, "I couldn't do it. But if you have three blue cards, you need to block Gloria from taking that route. Otherwise she's pretty much guaranteed to win the game." Depending on their relationship, Gloria could either get annoyed by Harry's comment (and would be well within her rights to do so) or she might playfully point out that he's twenty-three points ahead on the score track.

In a few games, like Liar's Dice, table talk is not only acceptable, it's essential. Liar's Dice is a raucous game in which players roll five dice and keep the result secret. Through a series of bluffs, they try to cause their opponents to lose dice by misjudging what the group as a whole has rolled. Throughout the game, lies are expected and an ongoing discussion about the odds of a certain outcome is assured. Calls of "You *have* to challenge him on that bid!" and "There's no way she has three wilds!" are part of the fun. Liar's Dice without table talk is inconceivable.

Likewise, a game like Bang!, a card game in which one player is known to be the sheriff but the identity of every other player is unknown, can't possibly be played without rampant table talk. The whole point of the game is for the sheriff to identify the deputies and the outlaws. Many social deduction games, like The Resistance and One Night Ultimate Werewolf, are also in this category.

Some games, especially those with cooperative elements, include rules specifically addressing table talk. For example, the rules of Pandemic say, "When playing the introductory game, place your cards faceup in front of you, for all players to see. When playing the standard or heroic games, keep your cards private, so everyone has information to contribute to play discussions." Thus, in a game with beginners, wide-open table talk is encouraged. Once players have some experience, table talk is still appropriate—but the hidden cards help prevent one person from dominating the decision-making. (The rules of Pandemic also say that experienced players may choose to play with faceup cards.)

You'll find discussion about the acceptable level of table talk in many game forums at BoardGameGeek. Within these conversations, people tend to have varying opinions; many of those opinions are strongly held.

In the end, whether trash talk or table talk is acceptable depends on two things: the game being played and the people playing it. You might be called on to arbitrate a dispute about one or both. You'll be better prepared to do that if you've thought about the issues in advance.

POST-EVENT WRAP-UP

As the host, your job doesn't end until the last guest leaves. And even then you have some post-event tasks to consider. I won't pretend to have any useful knowledge about cleaning up—I tend to put the games away (or at least into their boxes; I don't always make it down to the basement to put them back on the shelves), throw the dishes into the sink, and head to bed. But if you host a regular game night, it's a good idea to send a post-event wrap-up within a day or two. It doesn't have to be lengthy or detailed; something as simple as "Thanks for coming by last night! Don't forget we're getting together again in two weeks—hope to see you!" can work. But going the extra mile can help make your game night stand out, and it's more likely that your guests will come again if they know what to look forward to next time. That's doubly true if it's a special event that only happens once or twice a year.

For an annual game day that Beth and I have hosted since 2005, The Saturday Before Super Bowl Sunday Game Day (which will be discussed in more detail in chapter 6), I created a website at tsbsbsgd .wordpress.com. TSBSBSGD features a Battleball tournament, and the website tracks the history of that tournament. After the event ends, I highlight the winner in an article, post the completed bracket, add to the Hall of Champions, and update the complete player-versus-player results spreadsheet. (Maintaining the website also ties in to my love of useless statistics.) A friend, Josiah Fiscus, updates customized Battleball Power Rankings that are used to determine the tournament seeds. The website provides a sense of history and lends a fun feeling of pseudo-importance to an event that is, if I'm forced to admit it, quite silly.

Steffan O'Sullivan does a masterful job of sending out session reports after his game days. These are about six or seven paragraphs long and include brief summaries of the games played, such as this rather grisly one of Robinson Crusoe: "As it turned out, we lost, and it was because of my action! We desperately needed food, so I went hunting even though we had just failed at attempting to make defensive weapons. I was hoping to get a goat or some birds and unfortunately when the beast was revealed, I found myself trying to kill a gorilla who ripped my head off."

Not everyone sends post-event wrap-ups, but they can be a great way to further solidify the relationships being built at your game nights.

Great Games for Extra Large Groups

CATCH PHRASE

Four to twenty players
Designed by Craig Clark Williamson
Published by Hasbro (2000)

This game, once known as Electronic Catch Phrase, works well with a variety of player counts. Everyone sits in a circle, and every other player is on the same team. (If you have an odd number of players, you'll need to account for that—the easiest option is to have lopsided teams.)

The goal is for the person holding the electronic gizmo to get their team to guess a word or phrase by describing it. The describer has a few limitations. They can't say the word, try to rhyme it, or give any of the letters in the word. Otherwise, they're free to use verbal clues and gestures to their heart's delight. If a word proves too tough, the describer can skip it, but that wastes time—and you only earn a point if the timer buzzes when the gizmo is being held by the other team. The first team to earn seven points wins.

Let's go back to the timer. When a round starts, the timer beeps about once per second, a constant reminder to keep things moving. As the round progresses, the beeps speed up, adding wonderful doses of tension and pressure. The timer is not your friend.

In the standard game, several categories of words are available, such as Entertainment, Everyday Life, and The World. There are also themed versions of Catch Phrase, including *Star Wars*, Music, and Decades.

CONCEPT

Four to twelve players
Designed by Gaëtan Beaujannot and Alain Rivollet
Published by Repos Production (2013)

When Concept's colorful game board is first laid out on the table, you might think you're looking at some kind of graphic design template. You'll see arrows; shapes; a smiley face and a frowny face; icons representing people, animals, and the weather; and much more. It's the foundation for an inventive and fun game that rewards creative thinking.

Each round, two players work together, trying to get another player to guess their secret word or phrase. First, the team draws a card and selects one of the words, names, or phrases on the card. There are three levels of difficulty: easy (*squirrel*), medium (*Bilbo Baggins*), and hard (*hungry like the wolf*).

The team gives clues by placing various markers—including a question mark, exclamation points, and simple cubes—on or near the icons on the board. When a player guesses correctly, that player and both members of the team score points. (Many people don't keep score in Concept, preferring to enjoy the game as a pure activity.) The 124 icons on the board provide a remarkable amount of flexibility, and clever placement of the markers will allow players to guess words and phrases that initially seemed impossible.

TWO ROOMS AND A BOOM

Six to thirty players
Designed by Alan Gerding and Sean McCoy
Published by Tuesday Knight Games (2013)

In this social deduction game, players are divided into two rooms, where they each receive a random card identifying both their team and individual character. One team (blue) counts the President among its members. The other team (red) includes the Bomber. At the start of the game, nobody's sure who their teammates are, so there's a lot of suspicion.

The first job in each room is for the players to choose a room leader. The game consists of a series of timed rounds. At the end of each round, the leaders will arrange a hostage exchange, so the makeup of each room changes—and, potentially, new leaders will be chosen.

At the end of the game, everyone reveals their card. If the President is in the same room as the Bomber, the red team wins. Otherwise, the blue team wins.

There's much more to Two Rooms and a Boom, though, because it includes more than a hundred cards (e.g., con man, immunologist, and tinkerer) that introduce exciting new powers and twists. And a bit of great news: the publisher has promised that the print-and-play version of the game will always be free. Simply download it from their site, print it out, spend some quality time with a pair of scissors, and you're ready to go.

ULTIMATE WEREWOLF: DELUXE EDITION

Five to seventy-five players
Designed by Ted Alspach
Published by Bézier Games (2014)

Werewolf is a public domain game and you can easily find card sets available to download and print. That's a great way to play. But Ted Alspach loves the game, and he added legions of features not available anywhere else to Ultimate Werewolf: Deluxe Edition.

Let's start with the basics. There are villagers and werewolves, and the two sides don't get along. Over a series of days and nights, villagers will try to identify and kill the werewolves, while the werewolves go about their business of killing villagers. The game is run by a moderator, and it ends when all members of one side have been eliminated. (While Ultimate Werewolf: Deluxe Edition works with up to seventy-five players, every player added to the game causes it to last a little longer, so a seventy-five-player game would take a very long time.)

The Deluxe Edition includes more than forty unique roles on seventy-eight role cards plus a scorepad for the moderator. If you enjoy Werewolf, you might want to consider the Artifacts expansion (giving each player an artifact with a special power), the Classic Movie Monsters expansion (the Blob, Frankenstein's Monster, and more), or the other available expansions. Ultimate Werewolf Legacy, a separate game, allows players to tackle a campaign-style version of Werewolf.

WELCOME TO . . .

One to one hundred players
Designed by Benoit Turpin
Published by Deep Water Games (2018)

Players in Welcome To . . . get the chance to plan a 1950s subdivision, complete with pools and parks. It's a delightful puzzle.

At the start of each turn, cards are revealed to create three sets, each with a house number and an action. Each player must choose one of the sets, write the number on their board (remembering that houses must be numbered in ascending order), and take the action. Potential actions include: build a fence, increase house values, duplicate a house number, and construct a pool or park.

In each game, three city plans are made available, and the first player to complete each one receives a bonus. Points are also scored for parks, pools, and other features. The game continues until one player has completed all three city plans, filled in all their houses, or had three turns where they couldn't use any of the number/action sets.

Welcome To . . . presents players with the interesting challenge of building their neighborhood using the same supplies as their opponents. Good planning skills are a must to master the puzzle. There's also some luck involved; sometimes you need the right number/action set to come up at the right time. Welcome To . . . plays quickly, and everyone stays involved in the game because all players do something in each round. Also nice is the fact that any number of people can play as long as each has a copy of the scoresheet. Several expansions, including the zombie-themed Outbreak and the less-terrifying Winter Wonderland, give Welcome To . . . even more staying power.

6

Game Days

Game nights are great, but full game days are one of my favorite ways to gather and enjoy board games with friends. The extended hours allow us to dig into whatever games we want while also spending plenty of time socializing and catching up. I'm talking about eight or more hours, anywhere from a handful to a hundred attendees, and significantly more planning than is needed for a typical game night.

Which segues into a simple reality you need to be aware of: as your event grows, you're likely to spend more time on administrative and organizational issues and less on actually playing games. We discussed that a bit in chapter 4, but it's even more true when you host a full game day. Andy Matthews of Meeple Mountain, which (among other things) hosts large game events in Nashville, Tennessee, says that he often doesn't sit down to play a game until more than two hours after an event begins. Before then, he says, "I walk up and down taking pictures of the event to upload to Facebook, I talk to people, and I offer to teach games that I know." And that's after arriving early to set up the space.

Still, once you get the hang of it, game days can be incredibly rewarding. As I mentioned in the previous chapter, Beth and I host an annual game day on the day before the Super Bowl. Logically enough, we call it The Saturday Before Super Bowl Sunday Game Day (or, for those who can't get enough of acronyms, TSBSBSGD). Two years before we first held this event, Hasbro (via its Milton Bradley imprint) published a football-themed game called Battleball. Designed by Stephen Baker and Craig Van Ness, Battleball is a tremendously fun, futuristic game modeled after American football. Games take about thirty to forty-five minutes, and there's a boatload of dice rolling so it's hard to take it too seriously. For sixteen years now, TSBSBSGD has been home to the Battleball World Championship. (It may not be "official," but I'm unaware of any competition for the title—and we have trophies.)

The Battleball tournament is nominally the focus of the event, but the truth is that most people who attend play either one game of Battleball (it's a single-elimination tournament) or none at all. Most of their time is spent playing some of the many other games that attendees bring and make available to everyone. In 2020, eighteen people entered the tournament, down slightly from twenty the year before but still the second most ever. In the first few years, anywhere from six to eleven people entered.

Some of our guests have been very consistent about attending; roughly a dozen people have entered more than half of the Battleball World Championship tournaments. But part of what gives TSBSBSGD its energy is the fact that new people are constantly joining us. Our invitation policy is simple: if you've attended before, you're invited—and you're welcome to invite someone else as long as you let me know in advance. (We're fortunate in that no one has done anything to be disinvited yet.)

WHERE TO HOLD THE EVENT

We held the first TSBSBSGD at our home and were joined by about a dozen friends. The event quickly outgrew our space, but luckily a friend worked for a local nonprofit that had a large room available. We held TSBSBSGD there for several years while it grew to between twenty-five and thirty attendees. (For a few of those years, a separate part of the building hosted a pigeon show while we played games. Sadly, the only ranked pigeon game in BoardGameGeek's database is a children's game, so there wasn't much opportunity for crossover.) When the nonprofit decided to sell the building, we had to find a new home for the event. A local public radio station where I worked in the early 1990s had a community room that could be rented out and happened to be perfectly sized for TSBSBSGD.

The community room is a wonderful location, and the people at the radio station are great to work with. If you're fortunate enough to find a place like that, however, don't let yourself become so comfortable with the arrangement that you neglect the basics. In 2020, I forgot to check in with my contact at the station until a few days before the event. When I did, he got back to me immediately—with bad news. Somehow my reservation never made it into the system, and they had rented the facility to another group. After a few hours of frantic emails and phone calls trying to find an alternative facility on essentially zero notice, the folks at the radio station came through for us by locating a local golf club with an open ballroom. It turned out to be a perfect setup since all we really needed were some tables and chairs, lights, a few outlets to plug in slow cookers, and access to bathrooms. Not every facility will be as good to work with as that radio station—they recognized their error and went above and beyond to fix it.

I've never signed a contract with any of the locations for our game days. That's a bad decision on my part. A more formal arrangement like that has many benefits, including the fact that it should spell out what happens if one side or the other has to cancel at the last minute. Although it may sound hollow in the do-as-I-say-not-as-I-do sense, having a contract is the right way to go.

Other options for game-day locations include a church with a good fellowship hall, which is where Jim Carvin hosts his annual Black Friday game day. "Find a good location that has late hours, lots of tables and chairs, and room for growth," he says. Jim uses Facebook, Meetup, and the BoardGameGeek Guild system, along with some personal invitations, to let people know about his game day.

You might be able to rent out a local fire hall at a reasonable price, and any hotel with a decent-sized meeting space can host a game day. Depending on the exact dimensions, a meeting room of about eleven hundred square feet should be able to comfortably accommodate a game day with up to fifty attendees. One benefit of working with a hotel is that they'll set up all the tables and chairs for you. A layout commonly known as "classroom" or "schoolroom" is the closest to what works best for a game day, but you'll have to ask for additional tables along the walls where people can share their games. Most facilities provide rectangular tables, but depending on the exact nature of your event, you might want to consider some circular tables. Be aware of size, though, if you take that approach: the circular tables available at many hotels are sized for eight to ten people eating a meal, not four to six people playing a board game. Whatever facility you choose, be sure to visit it in person before signing the contract so you can envision your game-day setup and share that vision with your contact.

Depending on the cost of the venue, you may decide to charge people to attend. That's not uncommon, nor is it rude. If you do that, be up front with guests about the costs when you invite them, provide a way to pay electronically, and establish a process to pay at the door. Enlisting an assistant or two for the latter job is a good idea, because you will inevitably get pulled away throughout the day. You'll also need to track who's paid and who hasn't.

FOOD FOR A GAME DAY

There are four basic ways to handle food during a game day, and we've done them all: provide the food yourself, organize group takeout orders, go with potluck, or let everyone fend for themselves.

At the high end of the service scale, providing all the food for your guests yourself will stand out and be memorable. That works best for game days with up to a dozen guests. At some TSBSBSGDs, we combined this approach with a sort of minipotluck system. We ordered large subs from a local deli and provided bottled water and other drinks, while others brought snacks. In some cases, we ordered a variety of pizzas, a popular option at game days.

For more recent TSBSBSGDs, we supplied bottled water, along with paper plates, plastic utensils, and paper towels, and encouraged everyone to bring food and additional beverages, full-on potluck. If you do go potluck, letting people announce what they plan to bring is key. We've found that starting a food thread on the Facebook event page is enough to prevent duplicate offerings. It's also wise to encourage people to focus on foods that can be eaten without utensils or those that only require one utensil.

Slow-cooker foods are always popular at potlucks, but be aware that many common options, such as stews and chili, can be messy. Other slow-cooker choices, like meatballs, can be eaten on buns and rolls, which helps minimize (but doesn't eliminate) the risk of spilling food on someone's game. Veggie trays, fruit trays, and charcuterie trays also work well at potlucks and have the benefit of being mostly game-friendly; the same is true of brownies, cookies, plain tortilla chips, and pretzels. If you have any chips, it's a good idea to have a couple of dips available. I won't presume to tell you whether a lemon dill hummus or a spinach artichoke dip is better than a classic salsa or guacamole, but people like their dip. (Strike that. I will presume: classic salsa for the win.) And, although accidents can happen, dip is a relatively safe game-day flavor builder. Some great guests go all out and bring everything needed to build burritos or enchiladas. If you have a guest like that, invite them back!

No matter what approach you take to feeding your guests, have plenty of napkins and paper towels on hand. You may regret not having enough, but you'll never regret having too many. The same is true of paper plates and plastic utensils. If you've opted to host your event at an outside venue, don't forget to make sure at least one large recycling bin and trash can will be available—and ask where they keep extra garbage bags. You might be surprised how much recycling and trash a group of gamers can create over the course of a day.

While I discussed my reasons for preferring bottled drinks earlier in the book, using disposable cups can work. One issue with them is that people lose track of which cup is theirs and you may wind up with a veritable minefield of half-full cups sitting around. Emptying the cups and throwing them away is an ongoing and wasteful process. Providing a few permanent markers near the cup supply allows guests to personalize their cups and reuse them throughout the day.

Food safety is an often overlooked, but vital, consideration at game days. Many gamers I know—I'm putting this kindly—don't focus on food safety, and you don't want to be responsible for people getting sick at an event you host. Two important tips:

First, be sure to wash your hands thoroughly (hot water and soap for at least twenty seconds) before handling any food. Additionally, keep at least one bottle of hand sanitizer near the food. Playing board games and card games necessarily involves touching surfaces (like plastic miniatures, cardboard pieces, and cards) that other people are also touching, so gentle nudges to encourage cleanliness are always smart.

Second, keep stuff in the refrigerator. If you don't have access to a refrigerator, use an ice chest. Anything perishable—think subs, sandwiches, dips, and pizza—needs to be chilled before it turns into a welcome mat for bad bacteria. Options for extending the life of such foods include placing them on a bed of ice or taking a little bit out of the refrigerator at a time. The U.S. Department of Agriculture recommends throwing away any meat or other food that should be refrigerated once it has been at room temperature for more than two hours. If possible, have someone help with this task since you'll have plenty else to do (including, hopefully, playing a few games).

WHO BRINGS THE GAMES?

Every game day I've organized or attended has operated on the honor system in terms of sharing games. One or more walls are lined with tables specifically reserved for games brought by the attendees; some people bring a few games, others bring dozens, and some don't bring any at all. Any game on those tables is available for anyone to play. It should be immediately apparent that this system can only work if everyone understands the Golden Rule of Game Day: "Treat your neighbor's games as you would have them treat yours."

To help everyone get their own games back at the end of the day, supply name tags or masking tape to put on the table and mark a general area as, for example, "Clarke Hinkle's Games." That makes it more likely that the people who borrow games remember where to return them. Anyone bringing games should put a business card, a sticker, or something else that includes at least their name and email address inside their games. Keep some index cards or sticky notes handy for anyone who doesn't.

Although few games are actually stolen at game days, they have been known to get returned to the wrong piles no matter how many steps are taken to prevent that from happening. Also, pieces can fall to the floor and be found later. It's a good idea to dedicate space on one table as the lost and found area. At the end of the day, take everything remaining in the lost and found home with you and send photos to your guests to identify the rightful owners.

TOURNAMENTS

At a game day, it's easy to arrive with a group of friends and continue to play games with that same group the entire day. Nothing's inherently wrong with that, but for many people one of the joys of game day is making new friends. The difficulty is that it takes actual effort to break out of your normal group because when you finish playing a game with three friends, the most natural thing in the world is to play another game with those same three friends.

As a host, one of your jobs is to keep the event entertaining. If your game day turns out to be a bunch of separate groups each essentially participating in their own game day, it won't last. One of the reasons TSBSBSGD continues is that people have made new friendships, and the one day a year they get together with those friends is the day before the Super Bowl.

A tournament, as it turns out, is a fantastic way to make sure people are meeting new people. For example, at TSBSBSGD, the Battleball World Championship seeds are determined based on previous performance in the tournament, but it might as well be random. (For most of the tournament history, it was.) More than two hundred games of Battleball have been played over the course of sixteen tournaments, and only one pair of players has faced off five times. In other words, a lot of Battleball games are being played by people who don't know each other very well.

There's always a chance that a tournament can become too competitive, even when the prize is an inexpensive trophy. One way to keep things low-key is to choose a game that practically insists on being casual, a game that actively fights against intense competitiveness. Battleball has two of the key ingredients: dice-based gameplay and a short playing time. (It's also a two-player game, which makes the tournament structure a breeze to set up. For a game with more than two players, you'll need to decide who advances—will it be the winner or the top two, or will you use some kind of a point system?) The more luck there is in a game and the less time it takes to play, the less chance that people will take a tournament too seriously. At the opposite end of the spectrum from Battleball: chess. No one will ever describe a chess tournament as low-key. (I'm not saying that Battleball doesn't reward tactical and strategic play. Far from it, as an in-depth analysis of the TSBSBSGD Power Rankings would prove. But it also features wildly improbable plays, dramatic come-from-behind victories, and more than its fair share of what-the-heck-just-happened? moments.)

Many games are perfectly appropriate for tournaments, but another that I've had personal success with is GoLo: The Golf Dice Game. Like Battleball, it's very luck-dependent and games are quite fast. The authors of a 2009 article in the *Journal of Statistics Education* ("How LO can you GO? Using the Dice-Based Golf Game GOLO to Illustrate Inferences on Proportions and Discrete Probability Distributions") found that "nearly everyone finds the game intrinsically interesting. The variety in the dice and the connection to a competitive sport make the game more interesting than something like Yahtzee where the dice have identical faces." Hosting a GoLo tournament during The Masters or one of golf's other major events is a natural game-day event.

At a smaller game day and with a quick-playing game like GoLo, consider a round-robin rather than a single-elimination tournament. In a round-robin, every player faces off against every other player one time. The winner is the person who won the most games; ties can be broken with head-to-head matches. Due to the number of games to be played, I wouldn't recommend a round-robin for any game that takes longer than twenty minutes or any more than seven players.

HOW TO ORGANIZE A GAME-DAY TOURNAMENT

- Choose a quick-playing, two-player game.
- Choose the style of tournament you prefer.
- Gather the names of everyone who wants to play— and don't pressure anyone.
- Set the brackets using a service like PrintYourBrackets .com or BracketHQ.com.
- Once it starts, keep the tournament moving.
- Give the winner a small trophy or medal.

To understand how appealing a tournament can be, consider the World Boardgaming Championships, an annual event held at Seven Springs Mountain Resort in Seven Springs, Pennsylvania. In 2019, WBC boasted more than 150 board game tournaments ranging from marathon war games like Paths of Glory, which re-creates World War I and takes about eight hours to play, to the lighthearted—but strategic in its own way—Love Letter, which typically ends in less than half an hour.

If you're hosting an event with a tournament, make sure the tournament games keep moving at a good pace. During TSBSBSGD, I'm constantly checking in to see how close the games in progress are to finishing and making sure players know when the next round might start. Sometimes one side of the bracket will move faster than the other, so depending on the circumstances I may remind players of their upcoming match several times. Another key to an efficient tournament is to have a hard-and-fast deadline for arrival, such as: if you want to play in the Battleball tournament, you have to be on-site by 1 p.m. Without a deadline like that, the opening round can lumber forward like a rhinoceros in a marsh. Even one late arrival can slow things down for everyone else. As the host, it's your job to prevent that.

Another potential logjam: tournament participants who get involved in long games. People playing in the tournament should be gently encouraged to focus on shorter games, like some of those reviewed at the end of this chapter.

Finally, don't schedule a tournament unless you have enough copies of the game to keep the brackets moving quickly. For TSBSBSGD, I've acquired enough copies of Battleball through the years that no one else needs to bring any, but in general it's a good idea to ask your guests to bring copies of the game.

Great Games That Play Quickly

5-MINUTE DUNGEON

Two to five players
Designed by Connor Reid
Published by Spin Master Games (2017)

As the title indicates, the goal of this sometimes chaotic game is to escape a dungeon, and you only have five minutes to do it. Start by choosing one of the ten available characters, each of which has a unique power, and drawing five cards from the appropriate deck. After the players randomly build the dungeon from a separate deck, the clock starts counting down.

Working cooperatively, players use their cards to dispatch monsters and overcome obstacles by matching the required symbols—arrows, jumps, scrolls, shields, and swords. Some cards provide special powers, like a magic bomb (which counts as one of every symbol) and a divine shield (which allows you to pause the timer and collect your wits), but the dungeon holds nasty surprises as well—including the Sudden Illness, which forces everyone to immediately discard their entire hands. At the end of the dungeon, you'll find one of the five big bosses. It's okay to be nervous, but you must overcome the big boss to win and escape.

Also available is 5-Minute Marvel, where the dungeon theme is replaced with characters from the Marvel Universe, such as Captain America, Spider-Man, Black Widow, Squirrel Girl, and the team of Rocket and Groot.

IMPACT: BATTLE OF ELEMENTS

Two to five players
Designed by Dieter Nüßle
Published by Ravensburger (2018)

Take a pile of custom dice. Divide them up among the players. Give the players a small sloped arena as a target area. Tell them they can hit other dice and knock them about when they make their throw. Fun ensues.

There's more to Impact: Battle of Elements than that, but the sheer pleasure of pitching dice into the arena should not be discounted. Dice are thrown one at a time with players making a press-your-luck decision to stop or continue. When two or more symbols match, the player claims those dice and their turn is over. If any dice show blanks, they're removed from the game. If a player manages to clear all the dice from the arena through matches and blanks, the next player must roll all of their dice at once.

The last person with dice remaining wins the game—or the round, as there are rules to chain multiple games together, as well as variant rules for activating elemental powers. This portable and easy-to-teach dice game works well with all ages and has a small enough footprint to be played in a bar or a waiting room or at your kitchen table.

A Harry Potter–themed edition of Impact: Battle of Elements is also available.

MURDER ON THE COSMIC EXPRESS

Four to six players
Designed by Stephen Eckman
Published by Screech Dragon Studios (2019)

This five-minute social deduction game is set on the Cosmic Express, an interplanetary cruise ship. The president of the cruise line has been murdered and depending on the character you're randomly and secretly assigned, you may or may not want the murderer to be caught. Roles include the captain, undercover detective, murderer, accomplice, decoy, and butler.

Neither the captain nor the undercover detective knows who the other is, but they share a goal: to see that the murderer is arrested. The murderer and accomplice do not want the killer to be caught, while the decoy (for reasons known only to the decoy) wants to be arrested for the crime. The butler wants the murderer arrested—and to collect junk along the way.

After roles are assigned and weapons are distributed, the game opens with the murder phase. Here, the killer learns what the murder weapon is, which is crucial because they want to collect all the weapon cards showing the one used to commit the crime. During the one-minute investigation phase, players exchange weapon cards with one another. This allows them to trade information and potentially identify the culprit.

During the interrogation phase, the captain is identified and players briefly discuss what happened during the investigation. When the captain has heard enough, the game moves to the arrest. The captain sends one player to the brig, and everyone reveals their cards to discover whether the guilty party was properly identified. Murder on the Cosmic Express packs tremendous fun into a small box and a short amount of time.

TICKET TO RIDE: NEW YORK
TICKET TO RIDE: LONDON
TICKET TO RIDE: AMSTERDAM

Two to four players
Designed by Alan R. Moon
Published by Days of Wonder (2018, 2019, and 2020)

I've mentioned Ticket to Ride several times in this book for the same reason it's so popular: it's downright fun. Over the years, the family of Ticket to Ride games has expanded in numerous directions. There's the massive (in terms of box size) Ticket to Ride: Rails and Sails, the kid-friendly Ticket to Ride: First Journey, and an out-of-print expansion called Alvin & Dexter that lets you add a rampaging dinosaur and an invading alien to your Ticket to Ride games.

But for those times when you want the exquisite tension of Ticket to Ride but lack the time for a full game, Ticket to Ride: New York, Ticket to Ride: London, and Ticket to Ride: Amsterdam fit the bill. They have smaller numbers of vehicles: taxi cabs in New York, double-decker buses in London, and hand-pulled carts in Amsterdam. The maps are smaller as well, and each one adds a unique extra scoring mechanic to the board.

Each game plays in fifteen to twenty minutes, and while the designer managed to shrink the game, the full-bodied fun and excitement still abound. In some ways, the small boards make the game even more tense and competitive.

ZOMBIE DICE

Two to eight players
Designed by Steve Jackson
Published by Steve Jackson Games (2010)

If a game of Zombie Dice takes more than ten minutes, you're doing it wrong. Everyone's a zombie looking for the food zombies love best, brains, and avoiding the weapon that scares zombies the most, a shotgun.

The thirteen dice, representing your victims, are sorted into three difficulty levels: green (six), yellow (four), and red (three). Each die features some combination of brains, footsteps, and shotgun blasts. On a turn, you randomly choose three dice and roll them. Each brain symbol is worth a point and you may reroll any dice showing footsteps. If, for example, you roll two brains and a set of footsteps, you can either stop and score two points—with the turn passing to the next player—or you can set aside the brains, randomly choose two additional dice from the supply, and take your chances by rolling them along with the one showing the footsteps.

The ever-present danger is that any shotgun blasts are set aside, and if you roll three or more blasts, your turn ends without scoring any points.

The first player to score thirteen points wins, and if you're like me, you'll want to immediately play another game.

7

Game Weekends

A weekend of gaming with a select group of friends is a fantastic way to connect or reconnect. There's nothing quite like bringing friends together to relax around the game table and enjoy one another's company in the casual atmosphere that a full weekend provides, especially when everyone stays at the same location. Although outings like this take a significant amount of planning and are far less common than standard game nights, they offer benefits such as hanging out with your friends away from the game table, exploring unique locales, and diving into legacy and campaign games.

The Inn at Westwynd Farm, just outside Hershey, Pennsylvania, is a great bed and breakfast, perfect for a long weekend getaway. It's close to all the attractions of Hershey (the self-proclaimed, and for good reason, Sweetest Place on Earth), but it's also a working horse farm with beautiful wide-open spaces. For ten years, Beth and I hosted annual game weekends there, including consecutive game weekends where some people stayed during the intervening weekdays as well. We moved our event to the Inn at Westwynd Farm after first holding it at two other B&Bs over the course of five years. The original inn was within walking distance of our home, but it only had a small number of guest rooms. We moved to a somewhat larger nearby inn for a couple of years before finding Westwynd Farm, which has a dozen rooms and suites available. Some years, our group of twenty-five to thirty friends filled nearly the entire inn for ten days.

It must be said that my wife was the superstar of this event. Beth researched area B&Bs and visited a number of them before we settled on Westwynd Farm. She prepared delicious home-cooked meals that she delivered to the inn. (Years later, people still rave about her hearty beef stew and white chicken chili.) She supplied snacks and beverages and kept everything stocked. And on Saturday morning, she collected orders for soups, salads, and sandwiches from a local deli, picked up the food, and made sure everyone got exactly what they wanted for lunch.

When Beth and I decided to take some time off from organizing the event, many of the attendees continued gathering there every year on their own. That speaks to the uniqueness of the setting, but also to the friendships that evolved through the years. Many of our guests didn't know one another before we brought them together at the B&B. Christine Biancheria, an attorney from Pittsburgh, was at the forefront of this gang, who christened their event the Rogue Weekend. "I decided to continue it because I absolutely love the company of the people that go," she says. "It's one of the most fun events I attend with some of the nicest people I know." Amy Hager, a teacher who's married to my college roommate Mark, says, "We love the time away, the relationships that we formed with everyone that comes, and how relaxed and fun it always is. We didn't want to lose the connections with great people and knew that it was worth the effort to see everyone."

WHERE TO HOLD THE EVENT

Of course, you don't have to hold your game weekend at a B&B. There are many options to consider, each with pros and cons. Regardless of where you choose to host, there are a few things you'll want to look for in a venue: the basics of cost, travel distance, and number of bedrooms and bathrooms—but also the game-specific considerations of amount (and type) of common space and availability of tables and chairs. Jonathan Gilmour, who once rented out a castle in Ohio for a game weekend, says making sure there's plenty of gaming space is one of the most important details in planning a game weekend. Your own personal preferences will determine whether you want several smaller breakout-style rooms or one large gaming area.

Services like Airbnb and Vrbo, which allow users to rent out entire homes and have opened up a wide array of alternatives for game weekends, are one of the best ways to find a weekend getaway. They offer a great deal of flexibility in terms of location and accommodations, but it can take a significant amount of research to find a suitable house and you'll be responsible for all of your food.

Tamara Lloyd has used the service HomeAway about half a dozen times, making sure to set filters for location, price, and amenities that work for her group. "I loved it every time," she says. "I like HomeAway because you always get the full property and never share it with others." She and her friends have used it when staying in New York City; Cooperstown, New York; Clayton, New York; and Virginia Beach, Virginia. "I very much enjoy a few days away from my normal area," Tamara says. "We have time to bond over seeing new sights, making meals together or going to restaurants, playing games, and having a few drinks together."

One issue unique to gamers is our need for multiple tables. If you have a group of eight friends staying together for a long weekend, but the Airbnb only has one table and it only seats six . . . well, that won't work. "Airbnb has a filter for number of bedrooms, but not number of dining room tables," says James Nathan, who has organized multiple game weekends. He was able to convince a potential Airbnb host to let him look at the house ahead of time.

James also rightly points out that the event organizer has to deal with the gritty details like assigning rooms and collecting payment. In his case, some attendees were locals and went back to their own homes each night while others were from out of town and stayed at the Airbnb. "How do you structure the price?" he asks. In my view, the only answer to that question is for the organizer to make the decision they think is most fair and then stick to it. In terms of bedroom assignments, I recommend a seniority-based system, allowing people who have attended for longer to choose ahead of those who are newer to the event.

John Kerr, founder of the Arlington (Virginia) Boardgamers, has been planning annual gaming weekends since 2005. On average, he hosts nineteen people and early on established the fact that this was a gaming getaway that happened to be at the beach (it started at the Outer Banks), not a beach vacation that happened to feature some gaming. He encouraged the guests to look at it as "a chance for Arlington Boardgamers (and extended Arlington Boardgamers) to game and spend time to get to know each other more."

John was familiar with the Outer Banks from family vacations and knew that rental houses, as opposed to hotels, were common there. Once the group outgrew their first house, they decided they were willing to pay a bit more for a location on the beach. Before choosing a specific house, John thought through some requirements. "The main criteria we had at first were that each bedroom had its own bathroom, each bedroom was suitable for two adults to share, and the living space was geared toward community gaming." What he means by "community gaming" is that his group wanted one large room that could serve as "a universal gathering and gaming space" rather than several smaller rooms. "With time," he says, "we also found out we valued some other amenities, such as being on the beach, the hot tub, and the theater room."

Despite the event's focus on gaming, John says the weekends are casual and people spend a little more than half the day playing games. "Game days and gaming events tend to be focused on gaming, which is great," he says. "But the more chill atmosphere of beach week is a nice change to that. I like that it feels more like a community than it does a group of folks getting together for gaming."

For Anye Shafer, who hosted a number of women-only events known as "Nobody But Us Chicks," one of the benefits of renting a house is the ability to cook meals and split the costs. "Other than any airfare, it was pretty reasonable," she says. "We always have a good time. Combination slumber party and game convention."

Steffan O'Sullivan and two friends once rented a cabin in Kōke'e State Park, Hawaii. "We did Hawaii stuff during the day, then played board games all evening," he says. "It was heavenly!" On another occasion, he got a great deal on a cabin on a lake in New Hampshire and filled all eleven beds for a weekend. "Some were using the canoes and kayaks while others gamed," he says. "But lots of people just read, swam, or walked around—rural New Hampshire is beautiful."

The main limitation to renting a house or cabin is the size of your group—anything more than eight people or so will require a large property. On the other hand, hotels can easily accommodate a larger group—though they tend to be less casual, and since your rooms will probably be in different areas and on different floors, the opportunities to fortuitously bump into one another will be limited. Also, you'll probably have to pay a separate fee to reserve meeting space at a hotel. A large bed and breakfast can be a good happy medium.

Finally, you might want to check with local organizations that have event halls—fire stations, churches, schools, and fraternal orders—to see if you can rent a space there. If you find such a location that works well for gaming, one option is to allow your guests to find their own accommodations nearby.

With some determined research, you're sure to find a great place to host a game weekend with your friends and family.

NEGOTIATING WITH THE VENUE

If you go with a service like Airbnb or Vrbo, little or no negotiation is required beyond asking the host any questions you might have. But as the event organizer, you should dive into the small print. Some available spaces may not allow parties, and you need to understand exactly what those restrictions entail.

"My advice is to be absolutely sure that you are protected in case your guests cause any damage to the space," says John Garnett, a veteran host. "If you're renting a house or other space, protect yourself by documenting the condition of the space prior to your rental. One way to do this is with a video camera with the owner's agent present. It's not like gamers tend to be huge party animals, but it's very easy to scratch a hardwood floor by moving tables around or scooting chairs back while sitting in them."

If you choose a bed and breakfast or boutique hotel for a game weekend, some discussions will be necessary. Our deal with the bed and breakfast was simple: they held a block of rooms for our group for an agreed-to period of time, after which they opened any remaining rooms to the public at large. They also cut back on the dining area decorations, since after breakfast we used those tables for games and it's hard to play games when there's a lace doily and a flower arrangement in the middle of the table. When non-gamer guests stayed in a room near the gaming area, we had to limit the noise starting at 10 p.m. We also had to be sure the tables were clear at the end of each night so breakfast could be served in the morning, but the innkeepers let us store our games in plastic tubs around the edge of the dining room. The innkeepers supplied two large garbage cans, one for recycling and the other for trash, because their dining room ordinarily only has a single small waste can. (It's not often used for multiday gatherings like ours.) They were happy to oblige and made sure that the trash and recycling were emptied regularly.

The Inn at Westwynd Farm provides some beverages and snacks to guests as a matter of routine, but if you book a B&B or hotel where that's not the case, you should confirm that you can bring your own. Something as simple as a cooler full of ice and bottles of water might be all you need, but Beth often provided goodies with a local flair. Since we live in central Pennsylvania, there are plenty of potato chips to choose from (Grandma Utz's are the best, followed closely by Martin's and Dieffenbach's). She also picked up cheeses and deli salads from area farmers markets and sweets from some of the many candy makers in the area. Our guests also devoured healthier options such as veggie trays and fruit salads.

PACING THE WEEKEND

Some of your guests won't be interested in much other than playing games, eating, and sleeping, while others will want to mix things up with outside activities. I've seen players stay at the game table for ten or more hours straight, even ordering food from a local restaurant that delivers to avoid missing any precious gaming time. But most people are a little more, shall we say, rational. They'll want to get some fresh air and visit a few local attractions since, after all, you can play games anywhere. If you're going to the effort of organizing a game weekend, why not take in the local color? Events unrelated to gaming will make your gaming weekend shine and have your guests clamoring to return.

I recommend organizing some activities in advance—a wine tour or pub crawl, perhaps, or a trip to an escape room. As long as you get some input from your guests and don't pressure anyone to attend, it's much easier to have a single person—you—setting a schedule than it is to get the group to agree on anything. If you'd rather have a more laid-back feeling, put together a collection of links to area attractions and send it to your guests a few weeks before your event so they can set their own schedules. For our guests at the bed and breakfast, Beth prepared detailed lists of local attractions and area activities happening during our game event. Although the inn had some of that information available in the form of brochures, Beth put a personal touch on it. She knew our guests and their interests, so she was able to highlight the attractions and events most likely to appeal to them. This helped make our B&B gathering more appealing to couples where one of the two is much more into games than the other. When we attend a game event, Beth needs a crowbar to pry me out of my seat. But apparently some people like to interact with the outside world. Go figure.

If you don't already know in advance, you'll quickly get a sense of how much time your guests want to devote to gaming compared to other activities. As host, you should set a general tone starting with your invitation—let people know if you intend for the weekend to be focused more on games or other events, and if you'll be planning some group events or if it will be completely unstructured. Properly setting expectations goes a long way toward preventing disappointment.

Over time, our guests learned about the area and started planning their own side trips. One group liked to tour area breweries, others relaxed at the Hotel Hershey's spa—which features packages like a chocolate fondue wrap and a cocoa massage—while another guest arrived early to try his luck at the poker table of a local casino. I'm pretty sure he won more than enough to cover his room cost.

Outside excursions are a central component of the game convention Gulf Games, so much so that organizer Greg J. Schloesser puts together specific events to encourage people to arrive early and spend time together outside of the game room. (Although Gulf Games has grown to become a small convention, and we'll talk more about it in chapter 8, it feels like a large game weekend because those who attend are such a tight-knit group—a fact due in no small part to Greg's focus on non-gaming activities.) "I try to host the summer Gulf Games in locations that have plenty of sightseeing opportunities," he says. "I also want there to be numerous restaurants, preferably within walking distance or a very short drive."

Among his favorite excursions is the whitewater rafting trip a group of gamers took in the Smoky Mountains of Tennessee and North Carolina. "Leon Hendee, a longtime Gulf Gamer, was a rafting fan and guide in college, so he was by far the most experienced person on the journey," Greg says. "We hit one rough patch of rapids and the only person to fall in was, you guessed it, Leon!"

Another tour he'll never forget is the food tour of downtown Greenville, South Carolina. "I've been on many food tours, but none like this one," Greg says. "The owner of the tour company is also a Greenville historian, so as we walked to the five restaurants, he gave us a history of the town, buildings, and famous characters. By the time we left the second restaurant, we were all full—and still had three more to visit."

Ah, yes . . . food. Meals are a crucial consideration at any game weekend. If you're staying at an Airbnb-type house, decide in advance whether you want to provide all the food (and perhaps even cook it) or ask everyone in the group to bring certain items. If you provide the food, you can certainly ask your guests to chip in to cover the cost—but do so in advance to avoid any sour feelings. If your group likes to eat out, I strongly encourage you to make reservations. And if you have

Great Games for Game Weekends

BETRAYAL LEGACY

~~~~~~~~~~~~~~~~~

Three to five players
Designed by Rob Daviau
Published by Avalon Hill (2018)

In chapter 4, I mentioned my fondness for Betrayal at House on the Hill. Here, I'll describe my adulation for Betrayal Legacy—my all-time favorite game.

No other game has so perfectly combined luck and strategy, theme and mechanics, agency and narrative. From the first time the components are spread out on the table, players take themselves on a wild ride through the history of one very haunted house. Generations of families will return to this place decade after decade, century after century, and they will discover mostly terrible things.

If you're familiar with Betrayal at House on the Hill, you're familiar with the core mechanics of Betrayal Legacy. Things have been changed to make gameplay smoother and better. Fifty new haunts have been written. Legacy elements have been added, including the heirlooming of items. Few things are as enjoyable as claiming a pitchfork, then finding it in a later game and being able to take advantage of its full power because it is *your* pitchfork.

The primary thing that elevates Betrayal Legacy is its use of story. The players have storylines that develop over time, and the game has an overarching narrative that unspools in delightful and surprising ways that often pay homage to—and play with—the tropes of classic horror films. The home itself also becomes a character here. The original 1666 house expands through the years, occasionally with renovations and upgrades but mostly with tragedy and death. It becomes ever more haunted and terrifying.

Without descending into spoilers, there's not much more to say except that Betrayal Legacy is genius.

MY CITY

Two to four players
Designed by Reiner Knizia
Published by Kosmos (2020)

In My City, each player constructs a community across several generations, watching a small village grow into a burgeoning metropolis. This legacy-style game features engaging, fast-paced, and family-friendly gameplay over a twenty-four-game campaign, meaning the decisions you make in one game alter the course of future games.

The buildings you construct are represented by Tetris-like polyominoes. Each shape is on a different card, and each turn, a card is flipped and players all place the building in their community. Players score points for how much of their board they cover, so they have to be strategic in which pieces they place and where they play them. As in all good architectural ventures, landscaping is key: players are rewarded for not building over trees but penalized for not building over rougher terrains.

Each game lasts about twenty-five minutes, and the campaign is sorted into eight three-game chapters. Each game has slight rule variations—offering different goals, scoring opportunities, new pieces, etc.—that keep the game fresh. As you play the legacy campaign, a story emerges as your city progresses from its earliest days through industrialization.

The winner gets a reward at the end of each game, and those who didn't fare so well get some assistance for future games, most often in the form of additional landscape stickers. Of course, there's also a big winner at the end of the twenty-four-game campaign. To facilitate playing more games after the campaign ends, the flip side of each player's board is an "eternal" game—which roughly resembles game ten of the campaign—that can be played over and over again.

My City is remarkably simple, but remarkably fun, and it's likely you'll find yourself looking forward to chapter after chapter in what is one of Reiner Knizia's best games.

PANDEMIC LEGACY: SEASON 1

Two to four players
Designed by Rob Daviau and Matt Leacock
Published by Z-Man Games (2015)

The mash-up of Pandemic and the legacy-game concept jells so well that it's easy to forget how much work the designers had to put into creating it. The foundation of Pandemic Legacy: Season 1 is the original Pandemic, but as you play through this game you'll find yourself in some wildly unexpected territory.

It doesn't spoil anything to say that the "season" takes place over a year, with each game representing a single month. You'll play twelve to twenty-four times (twelve if you're perfect—but you won't be perfect; twenty-four if you struggle mightily, but even during struggles the game is fun), each month bringing with it new surprises. Some are big, some are small, but every surprise will make you smile, grimace, or rub your temples while you consider the ramifications. Occasionally all three at once.

As the game progresses, the rules, the board, the cards, and the characters chosen by the players will evolve. Some changes will benefit you and your team, but others will make success much harder to achieve. No other game I've played has taken me on an emotional roller coaster anything like Pandemic Legacy.

When you finish Season 1, you can dig right into Season 2. And waiting just beyond the horizon is Season 0, a prequel announced in July 2020. Let's go save the world!

RISK LEGACY

Three to five players
Designed by Rob Daviau and Chris Dupuis
Published by Hasbro (2011)

Before Risk Legacy, there were plenty of campaign-style games in which characters evolved, storylines developed, and decisions from earlier games impacted later games. Heck, that pretty much describes a roleplaying game. But this was the first game to carry the legacy name, the first board game in which the physical components—the board, the rulebook, the cards—change from game to game. Some cards are destroyed (actually ripped up!), some of the countries on the board are permanently changed when stickers are added to them . . . It was a revolutionary idea.

Based on the classic war game Risk, Risk Legacy can trace its genesis to a discussion at Hasbro, where designer Rob Daviau worked at the time. During a conversation about Clue, a Hasbro mainstay, Daviau joked that "they shouldn't keep inviting these people over to dinner because they keep murdering people." He wondered, "What if the game didn't fully start over each time? What if it had some sort of memory of what happened before?"

That led to the legacy concept, which has now been implemented—in one fashion or another—in more than fifty games, including some of the most highly regarded games ever published.

In an early comment about Risk Legacy on BoardGameGeek, my friend Brad Minnigh said this: "A new dawn of games is approaching." He was absolutely right. But Risk Legacy is more than the first legacy game. It stands on its own merits and takes Risk to new heights. If you have fond memories of playing Risk, give it a shot. You won't be disappointed.

STAR WARS: IMPERIAL ASSAULT

Two to five players
Designed by Justin Kemppainen, Corey Konieczka, and Jonathan Ying
Published by Fantasy Flight Games (2014)

My dad took me to see the original *Star Wars* movie in the theaters in 1977, and it blew me away. In recent years, fans of the galaxy far, far away have been treated to some amazing games. None is better than Imperial Assault.

The game comes with thirty-four plastic miniatures, including Luke Skywalker, Darth Vader, a host of stormtroopers and Imperial Guards, and an AT-ST. You can play in skirmish mode, basically a brawl in the *Star Wars* universe, or campaign mode, which is where Imperial Assault truly shines.

The forty-four-page Campaign Guide boasts thirty missions, many of which form an interconnected storyline. One player takes the role of the Empire while the others are part of the Rebel Alliance. Each mission has specific objectives for each side, but only the Imperial player has access to the Campaign Guide—as in the movies, the Rebels often have to act without full knowledge of what they're getting into.

If you want more Imperial Assault after making your way through the core game, or you'd like to add iconic characters like Han Solo and Boba Fett, explore the six major expansions (including Jabba's Realm, Return to Hoth, and The Bespin Gambit) and the dozens of available ally packs.

MORE GREAT GAMES FOR GAME WEEKENDS

AEON'S END LEGACY
one to four players, designed by Nick Little and Kevin Riley,
published by Indie Boards & Cards, 2019

CHARTERSTONE
one to six players, designed by Jamey Stegmaier,
published by Stonemaier Games, 2017

CLANK! LEGACY:
ACQUISITIONS INCORPORATED
two to four players, designed by Andy Clautice and Paul Dennen,
published by Renegade Game Studios, 2019

GLOOMHAVEN
one to four players, designed by Isaac Childres,
published by Cephalofair Games, 2017

THE KING'S DILEMMA
three to five players, designed by Hjalmar Hach and Lorenzo Silva,
published by Horrible Guild, 2019

8

Small Game Conventions

If you want to take your game day to the big leagues, you can turn it into a small convention. Local and regional game conventions all around the world bring together a wide diversity of gamers to enjoy time together at the table. Fair warning: this will take a *lot* of work. The most obvious difference between a small game convention and the other game events we've discussed is the increased number of attendees, which leads to many other issues. Once you have more than, say, twenty-five people attending, you're essentially running a small professional event. When people pay an entry fee—roughly $50 to $150 for the three small conventions discussed in this chapter—their expectations increase. Everyone's problems become your problems.

I recommend that you get comfortable hosting a large game day or weekend before trying your hand at a full-blown convention. If a comparable event is already established in your area, you may want to consider working with them instead of starting what could be a competitor. But if you do eventually decide to organize a game convention, the key is to start small and grow over time. And I would be remiss if I didn't encourage you to take a look at the event-management tools available at the website Tabletop.Events, owned by BoardGameGeek, which can help you deal with the many administrative issues you'll face.

START MINI, GROW TO SMALL

The Gathering of Friends, created by Alan R. Moon in 1990, started with twenty-three attendees. At the thirtieth Gathering in 2019, attendance reached 437. That's an average growth rate of about fourteen people per year. Alan began the event at the behest of some friends from the days when he worked at game publisher Avalon Hill in Baltimore. "For several years, they had been bugging me to organize a bigger event," Alan says. "I resisted for a long time but then, during a stretch when I had a lot of time on my hands, I relented. The initial idea was just a long weekend with a small group of friends."

Alan is one of the top game designers in the world, but that's not why the Gathering has become so popular. Because of the deep friendships forged among his guests over the years, people travel from all over the globe to Niagara Falls, New York, every spring. The Gathering is a can't-miss appointment on many people's calendars. He does a tremendous job of managing everything—he provides updates on the Gathering of Friends website (which is run by an attendee on a volunteer basis), serves as liaison with the hotel whenever any guest has a problem, organizes the Saturday morning flea market, enlists a team to fill the welcome bags, takes everyone who's still there to dinner on the final Sunday . . . the list goes on. Alan constantly adjusts the event to fit what his guests want. "People who come year in and year out look forward to it," he says. "And they leave with the event having met their expectations."

Craig Massey, who has helped organize a weekend-long event known as Lobster Trap near Boston each fall for the past twenty-two years, says anyone wanting to start a small convention would do well to aim for an event with ten to twenty good friends for the first year. "Put something on the calendar," he says. "Communicate regularly and stick to the plan. If game events are scheduled consistently, whether it's a weekly game night or an annual event, people will come and make it a priority—because you as the host make it a priority. If an event is held inconsistently and has poor communication, people find it easy to not participate."

Nearly two hundred people now attend Lobster Trap, and Craig says he invites about a dozen new people every year to maintain that size. "I'm constantly on the lookout for people who are fun to play games with," he says. "We want people who are easygoing, enjoy a variety of games, and are willing to share their games and passion for playing them. But it's never just about the games. It's about being with people whose company you enjoy."

Gulf Games, a small convention that takes place twice a year (in February and July), started as a way for people who had met online to extend their friendship to the real world. Greg J. Schloesser, Ted Cheatham, and Ty Douds decided to get together with their families in May 1998 in Navarre Beach, Florida, part of that state's panhandle.

"We had so much fun, we decided to do it again later that year," Greg says. "We invited a few other folks we either knew personally or chatted with online. We formally gave the second event a name: Gulf Games 2. That event had nine families, and we continued to grow from there!" The summer edition of Gulf Games now draws more than 160 people, and the social aspect is the event's linchpin. "Socializing and getting to know folks is one of my prime motivators in life," Greg says. "Gulf Games sprung out of that love of socializing and the desire to meet new folks. As such, I have always strived to give Gulf Games a fun, friendly atmosphere where folks can meet, socialize, game, and develop lifelong friendships."

WHERE TO HOLD THE EVENT

For a small game convention, you're almost certain to want the kind of conference space available in a hotel. Holding the event in a hotel also gives out-of-town guests a natural place to spend the night, and if people fly in for the event it may save some of them the cost of renting a car.

When Alan moved The Gathering to Niagara Falls, one of the considerations was proximity to his home. But that was far from the only one. "I wanted a nice hotel," he says. "I was done with the 'bargain basement' hotel in Columbus (Ohio) where The Gathering was for many years. I wanted some comfort and some perks. Most of all, I want a hotel that really *wants* to host my event. A hotel that values my efforts as an organizer and values the money I bring in to the hotel." Alan says he immediately developed a great relationship with the staff at the Sheraton in Niagara Falls, and it's grown better every year since.

Before deciding on a hotel, choose two to five contenders and visit them in person so you can visualize what the event will look like. Meet with the staff at the hotel who will be your contacts, especially those who will be in charge of helping should any issues arise during the event. Consider the needs of your guests: Will they be more interested in cost, amenities, or a good balance of the two? Some contracts may include a guaranteed minimum number of room nights, additional charges for modifying the meeting space beyond the initial setup, or other requirements. Before you sign a contract, be sure you understand all of its provisions.

"Usually everything is up for negotiation," Alan says. "The more room nights you're guaranteeing and actually bringing in, the more you should be able to get for free from the hotel. It never hurts to ask for things. In addition, if there are problems, it's good to keep a list of them and use these things to get concessions. But in general, if the hotel is a good fit, they will work with you to make the event a success because they want you to keep coming back."

For Gulf Games, Greg says the number of room nights generated by the event typically allows him to negotiate the cost of the meeting room down to "a reasonable onetime setup fee." While the event officially begins on Thursday, he holds a welcome party on Wednesday evening with some light food. "Hotels like this," he says, "and it helps in the negotiation."

DEALING WITH HARASSMENT AND OTHER SERIOUS ISSUES

The larger your event, the more likely you'll have to deal with problems related to player behavior. The Gathering of Friends retains an everybody-knows-your-name, superfriendly kind of feeling. Alan believes that's because of his focus on the invitation list, and I agree—but occasionally he has had to address the conduct of some attendees. "I don't put up with bad behavior," he says. "I haven't had to remove many people from the group, but I do it when necessary because I know that if I keep the bad apples, I could lose some of the good ones. So as hard as it is to uninvite someone, it has to be done."

Remember, *you* set the tone for your game event. Whether it's five or fifty or fifty thousand people, it is your responsibility to make it clear from the get-go—by your actions just as much as your words—that harassment, cheating, and other unwelcome conduct will not be tolerated. If you do that, you're far less likely to have a problem. For a small group of friends, there's no need to formalize a policy; it should be enough to establish and enforce a don't-be-a-jerk rule. For larger gatherings, it's wise to create a written policy and ensure that everyone who attends has read and understands it. Consequences should be clearly spelled out and proportionate to any offense.

Nearly seventy thousand people attend Gen Con in Indianapolis, Indiana. More than sixty thousand people attend PAX Unplugged in Philadelphia. Both have clear antiharassment policies, which can serve as good models for your own, posted on their websites.

Gen Con's antiharassment policy prohibits "any behavior that threatens a person or group or produces an unsafe or noninclusive environment." Depending on the circumstances, potential sanctions include being expelled from Gen Con, being banned from all future Gen Con events, and reporting the incident to the appropriate authorities. PAX Unplugged's policy is similar, allowing show management to revoke the attendance badge of anyone engaged in harassing or threatening behavior and potentially ban them from future events.

Unfortunately, such incidents do happen and before you host a group where you don't personally know everyone attending, you should be prepared with a policy that provides clear definitions and penalties. Taking that step before a problem emerges can save you a lot of trouble.

9

Themed Game Nights

Many tabletop games have no theme at all. Classic strategy games like Go, backgammon, and checkers are good examples, along with more modern games like Hex, Blokus, and Kris Burm's terrific series of abstract games known as Project GIPF. But most games published today have themes, meaning that the game is *about* something. Even if there's not a strong narrative component, players can envision themselves taking on a role beyond that of "person at the table moving bits around." Think of Clue, where every player is a specific character trying to solve the murder of Mr. Boddy (or Dr. Black if you're playing Cluedo in the UK).

Each year, BoardGameGeek invites its users to vote on a set of awards known as the Golden Geeks. One of those awards is presented to the Best Thematic Board Game. Winners include Gloomhaven, where players descend into dungeons to complete missions; Robinson Crusoe: Adventures on the Cursed Island, which requires players to find food, build shelter, create tools, and more; and Dune, based on the classic science fiction novel by Frank Herbert.

Jared Vento, who hosts weekly game nights, says themes can help attract new players. "Because we run a game night open to the public, we have to do a little bit of planning to keep interest from week to week," he says. "We feel that a theme has helped us do that."

Given the explosion of game titles over the past several years, there are good options for just about any theme you can think of. With a little work, you can cook up a themed evening of games that your friends will remember for a long time. You might try a food-themed game night, pairing tasty treats with games like Sushi Go Party!, Food Chain Magnate, Rival Restaurants, and New York Slice. (Perhaps avoid Cockroach Salad and Lord of the Fries.) Or, if you're feeling some cabin fever, book a travel night. I recommend you start with 10 Days in the USA, On Tour, and The Voyages of Marco Polo.

Some hosts go all out, adding theme-appropriate decorations and food to enhance the atmosphere. Vanessa Shannen-Anderson's friends arrive in costume when it's time to play *Star Wars* games or Dungeons & Dragons. She also hosts murder mystery parties and says, "There's a lot of prep, but you would be surprised at the people who play in character." Jeremy Thigpen also hosts costumed guests. "Sometimes," he says, "I ask players to come dressed in thematic clothing if we're playing a Sherlock Holmes–type game, or a game where theme is so prevalent and we'll be doing some character voices or roleplaying aspects."

Whatever theme you choose, commit to it! For many people, myself included, theme is central to why we love our favorite games. Taking the time to plan an entire game night around a specific theme is a great way to create a memorable event.

For a truly unforgettable game night, hire a tattoo artist to ink your guests while playing the party game Tattoo Stories. But if that's too extreme, try one of these ideas . . .

MYSTERY

Who doesn't love a good murder mystery? Crime has been a popular theme in board games even before the venerable classic Clue, which has been published in at least fifty editions since it debuted in 1949. One of the earliest mystery board games is Mr. Ree!: The Fireside Detective (1937), a game that almost certainly inspired the development of Clue.

This genre of games is packed with wonderful thematic choices beginning with the tremendous Detective: A Modern Crime Board Game (Portal Games, 2018). The base game comes with five cases to solve, and new cases continue to be published. The biggest downside to this cooperative game is the playing time of two to three hours, although a separate-but-related game—Detective: Season One—offers streamlined gameplay with each of its three standalone cases taking about ninety minutes.

Chronicles of Crime (Lucky Duck Games, 2018) uses a combination of a board game, an app, and a simple virtual reality experience to immerse players in a world of investigation and interrogation. It was nominated for five Golden Geeks, including Game of the Year and Most Innovative Game.

The Mystery Rummy series of card games, designed by Mike Fitzgerald, fits right in on a mystery-themed game night. The first game, Mystery Rummy: Jack the Ripper (U.S. Games Systems, 1998), was followed by Murders in the Rue Morgue, Jekyll and Hyde, Al Capone and the Chicago Underworld, and Escape from Alcatraz. As you likely deduced from the title, the mystery theme of these games is blended with a modified version of the traditional card game Rummy.

Agatha Christie's Death on the Cards (Modiphius Entertainment, 2019) consists of eighty cards and a lot of tension. Many of Christie's most beloved characters—such as Hercule Poirot, Miss Marple, Tommy and Tuppence, Mr. Satterthwaite, Harley Quin, and Lady Ellen "Bundle" Brent—play key roles in the game, enabling players to judge which among them is the murderer.

Other choices that can be enjoyed during a mystery-themed game night include Stop Thief (Restoration Games, 2017, a reworking of the 1979 classic), Sherlock Holmes Consulting Detective (published in numerous editions and expansions over the years), Deception: Murder in Hong Kong (Iello, 2014), Scotland Yard (Ravensburger, 1983), Mr. Jack (Hurrican, 2006), Witness (Ystari Games, 2014), and P.I. (Treefrog Games, 2012). One of the most unique is Mord im Arosa (Zoch Verlag, 2010), a surprisingly engrossing game that involves players dropping small wooden cubes (representing clues) into the top of a seven-story-tall cardboard building and trying to ascertain which floor they landed on.

NATURE

I received Parks (Keymaster Games, 2019) for Christmas and couldn't wait to play it with my wife, our sister-in-law, and our nephew. The gorgeous box cover promises beautiful art inside, and you won't be disappointed: the art is taken from the Fifty-Nine Parks Print Series. Gameplay is equally enjoyable, perfect for a game night with those who enjoy light strategy games. Each player controls two hikers trekking along trails through all four seasons of a year.

Speaking of beautiful games, Wingspan (Stonemaier Games, 2019) has garnered well-deserved attention since its release. Designer Elizabeth Hargrave created a wonderful strategy game centered around the hobby of birdwatching. That may sound strange, but it's true, and the game works on many levels. I'm a huge fan of Wingspan. Players strive to attract the best birds to their wildlife areas, and the game includes 170 unique bird cards, each with a striking illustration. By the way,

Wingspan isn't just great for game night; students studying birds will learn a ton while playing.

Continuing the theme of nature games, and that of spectacular art, are a trio of strategy games from North Star Games: Evolution (2014), Evolution: Climate (2016), and Oceans (2020). Each is dynamic with a theme that is inseparable from gameplay, so much so that the scientific journal *Nature* raved about Evolution when it reviewed the game. ("Evolution features sophisticated biology. Traits can be put together in a dizzying array of combinations, so each game can be very different. The theme of evolution is not just tacked on: it drives play.")

Fauna (Huch!, 2008) is an underrated gem. In each round, an animal is revealed and players set cubes of their color on the board—which includes a world map and three scales (weight, length, and tail length)—trying to claim positions relevant to the animal in question. Absolute precision is not required since players can earn points for placing their cubes adjacent to the correct answers.

The selection of nature-themed games is almost as vast as nature itself. Among the options are Photosynthesis (Blue Orange Games, 2017), Arboretum (Z-Man Games, 2015), Butterfly (Rio Grande Games, 2019), Habitats (Cwali, 2016), and Hive (Gen42 Games, 2000). If you've ever felt an urge to take up farming, check out the deep strategy game Agricola (Lookout Games, 2007) or the card game Bohnanza (Amigo, 1997). The unique process of adding cards to your hand and playing them to the table makes Bohnanza particularly fun and challenging.

FOOTBALL

My father grew up in Superior, Wisconsin, and was a lifelong fan of the Green Bay Packers. He passed his love of the team on to me, and now my wife and I are both part owners of the greatest franchise in the history of professional sports. So, yeah, I love American football. And although you may think of video games when it comes to football and other sports, there's a long history of great tabletop versions, too.

In chapter 6, I wrote about the Battleball tournament we host every year on the day before the Super Bowl. While Battleball feels an awful lot like you would expect football to feel if it were played by robotically enhanced humans, it's far from a simulation. For a game night featuring more realistic football-themed board games, you might want to dig into the past for either Football Strategy (originally published in 1959) or Sports Illustrated Pro Football (first published in 1970 and also released under the name Paydirt). In Football Strategy, for which the World Boardgaming Championships still holds a tournament every year, the offensive player chooses one of twenty plays and the defensive player chooses one of ten formations. The results of each play are determined by checking a matrix to see where those two choices intersect. Paydirt features team charts based on every team in the NFL, and although official updates haven't been published for decades, fans of the game continue to make new charts available online. If a game driven by statistics appeals to you but you prefer more modern teams, check out the Strat-O-Matic game company. Best known for its baseball game, Strat-O-Matic also publishes Pro Football with sets available for NFL teams as far back as 1956.

For some players, a detailed simulation like Strat-O-Matic Pro Football is the gold standard. (One reviewer at BoardGameGeek calls it "arguably the best head-to-head sports simulation game ever.") For me, however, games like 1st & Goal (R&R Games, 2011) and 1st & Roll (R&R Games, 2018) hit the sweet spot when it comes to football board games. Both games were designed by Stephen Glenn and they share much in common, including a wonderful magnetic board. 1st & Goal is primarily powered by cards (though there are plenty of dice); 1st & Roll relies even more on dice. Both are wildly entertaining for football fans. 1st & Goal includes a pair of sixty-card decks (one for offense, one for defense—each split evenly between running plays and passing plays) and ten dice (seven team dice and three game dice). After the kickoff, each player draws eight cards from the appropriate deck and chooses one to play. The cards are compared to determine which dice are rolled; the results on the dice decide the outcome of the play. 1st & Roll eliminates the cards and streamlines the game, allowing players to finish in about half the time.

Another good option is Football Highlights 2052 (Eagle-Gryphon Games, 2019), a sequel of sorts to Baseball Highlights 2045. It evokes the imagery of early twentieth-century football with leather helmets and no facemasks. There are no dice here, and each card choice affects a team's offense and defense.

SOCCER

To the rest of the world, football is the game actually played with your feet—soccer. My favorite tabletop soccer game is StreetSoccer (Cwali, 2002), which was later reworked as Champions 2020 (Cwali, 2011). StreetSoccer is played on a tight field, a ten-by-six grid, with five players (including the goalie) per side. Games are quick, about twenty minutes each, and full of tactical decisions. A six-sided die controls both movement and kicking the ball, but the game shines with a passing system that rewards players who cleverly position their team. Champions 2020 expands the StreetSoccer system to a much larger field and adds more options and decisions. For me, the smaller version is perfect.

Subbuteo (originally published in 1947) is a dexterity game played on a cloth board with miniature footballers on rounded bases. The minis are flicked in real time so players are constantly moving around the table to position themselves for the next shot. Planning ahead is rewarded, as it usually takes a series of passes to set up a good shot on goal. Although much more popular in Europe, where it's one of the classic tabletop games, Subbuteo has many die-hard fans in North America as well.

World Cup Tournament Football (Australian Design Group, 1993) is a dramatically different take on soccer games. Here, players complete an entire sixteen-team tournament in about an hour. The game starts with each player receiving five random teams, some more capable than others. Gameplay consists of adding cards, some helpful and some unhelpful, to the various teams in the tournament. When all cards have been played, they're revealed and the teams work their way through the bracket.

RACING

So many races, so little time! Whatever kind of race you're interested in, there's almost certainly a game for you. And if you want to take things to the next level, it's pretty simple to create ongoing leagues for most race games. I have two friends who host an annual Formula D (Asmodee, 2008) tournament with six regular players. The games take place every other week and as part of the stakes, the winner's favorite food is served at the next race.

Formula D, a new version of 1991's Formula Dé, appeals to race fans for many reasons. At the start of every turn, a decision must be made whether to shift gears (a series of custom dice represent the gears: a car only moves one or two spaces in first gear, but in sixth gear a car moves twenty-one to thirty spaces), allowing players to manage the reward of speeding along the track with the risk of taking a corner too fast and crashing. The many expansions (twelve additional tracks have been published for Formula D, and the older Formula Dé tracks can also be used) give the game plenty of variety.

Two other outstanding auto racing games are Downforce (Restoration Games, 2017) and Rallyman: GT (Holy Grail Games, 2020). Downforce combines a card-based racing system with the prerace decision of which car(s) to buy and several in-game decisions of which cars to wager on. The tracks in Rallyman: GT are created with a set of thirty-one double-sided hexagonal tiles, providing a ridiculous number of options. This game uses a unique dice-based movement system.

Horse racing has been a popular theme for board games for more than 150 years. One of the earliest was Game of Steeple-Chase, published in 1862 by McLoughlin Brothers. More modern entries include my favorite, Winner's Circle (Alea, 2001), Long Shot (Z-Man Games, 2009), and Horse Fever (Cranio Creations, 2009).

My favorite bicycle racing game, Um Reifenbreite (Jumbo, 1979), has long been out of print. Fortunately, used copies tend to be available on secondary markets like eBay and the BoardGameGeek GeekMarket. The English translation of the title is "By the Width of a Tire" and this award-winning board game simulates a Tour de France–style race. Flamme Rouge (Stronghold Games, 2016), Leader 1 (Ghenos Games, 2008), and Breaking Away (Fiendish Games, 1991) are all worthy bicycle racing games as well.

If none of those racing options appeal to you, perhaps you'd enjoy seeing who has the fastest horse-drawn chariot (Ave Caesar, 1989), the fastest hovercraft (Q-Jet 21xx, a harder-to-find remake of Ave Caesar), the fastest dogsled team (Snow Tails, 2008), or the fastest camel (Camel Up, 2014). For a top-notch game with a bit of tongue-in-cheek humor, find the fastest sloth with Fast Sloths (2019, designed by Friedemann Friese, one of the world's most creative game designers). Finally, get your hands on a copy of Pitchcar (1995) to see who can flick a wooden disk around a track with the best combination of finesse and power. Seriously, Pitchcar is tremendous fun.

HORROR AND HALLOWEEN

At the end of every October, gamers gather at tables around the world to fight off zombies and other monsters by playing games that truly evoke the spirit of Halloween. I wrote earlier about my love of Betrayal at House on the Hill and Betrayal Legacy, two of the very best games for such occasions. But they have plenty of company.

Horrified (Ravensburger, 2019) boasts detailed plastic miniatures of many of the most-loved monsters from Universal's vast movie archive: the Wolf Man, the Invisible Man, the Mummy, Dracula, the Creature from the Black Lagoon, Frankenstein, and the Bride. Working together, players try to rid the town—filled with locations like a mansion, police precinct, church, hospital, and a graveyard suspiciously close to the hospital—of the creatures. It's simple to adjust the difficulty level: an easy game uses two monsters, a standard game uses three, and a challenging game uses four.

Dead of Winter (Plaid Hat Games, 2014) thrusts players into a colony of survivors fighting against flesh-eating humanoids and, often, one another. There's one overall goal that everyone works toward (such as "find a cure") but each player also has a secret objective (like "hope"). Some objectives are relatively harmless to the group, but some involve betrayal, requiring the player to actively work against the group's interest. Dead of Winter is a Crossroads game, a style created by Plaid Hat. At certain points in the game, the players face choices—some decided democratically, some not—that create dramatic moments and can have a big effect on the game.

Zombicide (CMON, 2012) and Last Night on Earth (Flying Frog Productions, 2007, with a ten-year anniversary edition published in 2017) also find players defending themselves against zombies, but everyone's role is clear in both games: the cooperation is full-fledged. Both feature modular boards and multiple scenarios. One key difference is that in

Last Night on Earth, one player controls the zombies instead of a hero; in Zombicide, all players are heroes.

For my money, the best way to close out a Halloween game night is with One Night Ultimate Werewolf (Bézier Games, 2014), the quick-playing social deduction game reviewed in chapter 4. Other games in the series include One Night Ultimate Vampire, One Night Ultimate Alien, and One Night Ultimate Super Villains.

TRAINS

My father worked for Amtrak, my grandfather worked for the Soo Line, and my great-grandfather worked for the railroad in Norway, so trains are in my blood. No surprise, then, that I enjoy games with a railroad theme. My clear favorite is Ticket to Ride (Days of Wonder, 2004), which is reviewed in chapter 3. Among the various Ticket to Ride expansions, I'm partial to the Pennsylvania map—in part because of the geography (the Keystone State has been my home state for more than 90 percent of my life) and in part because it adds stock purchasing to the game. The Nordic Countries map is a close second.

Like Ticket to Ride, Union Pacific (Amigo, 1999) was designed by Alan R. Moon. This one focuses even more on the stock element than Ticket to Ride's Pennsylvania map, as players are constantly choosing between increasing a company's value or adding to their ownership of a company. It's all about the cash in Union Pacific.

Age of Steam (Warfrog Games, 2002) and Steam (Mayfair Games, 2009) are closely related, though you'll find plenty of gamers who swear by one or the other. In both games, players build tracks, upgrade their trains, upgrade cities, and acquire goods to be delivered. Both games have expansion maps available; most maps are compatible with either game.

Ted Alspach, head of Bézier Games, has created many of those Age of Steam expansions. His company also publishes its own great train games, Maglev Metro (2020) and Whistle Stop (2017). Maglev Metro features transparent tiles that allow you to build over other players' networks, while Whistle Stop adds interesting new elements to the basic Age of Steam structure (hex-shaped tiles and pick-up-and-deliver mechanics).

If you find that train-themed games make you want to get off your caboose and play more, other good options include Russian Railroads (Hans im Glück, 2013), Chicago Express (Queen Games, 2007), and Trains (OKAZU, 2012).

EVEN MORE THEMES

You can dedicate an entire game night to nearly any theme you think of. On Valentine's Day, Bayard Catron of Maryland likes to host a themed game night—the theme being anti-Valentine's.

If you want to put together a themed game night, here are a few more suggestions:

Superheroes: There are far too many excellent Marvel and DC games to list here, but other powerful options exist, including Sentinels of the Multiverse, Capes & Cowls: Adventures in Wyrd City, and One Night Ultimate Super Villains.

Politics: Those who enjoy politics (and many of those who don't) will vote for 1960: The Making of the President, Twilight Struggle, Die Macher, Watergate, 13 Days: The Cuban Missile Crisis, and Founding Fathers.

The Wild West: Strap on your six-shooter with Bang! (I prefer Bang! The Dice Game, which maintains the appeal of the original but shortens gameplay), Great Western Trail, Western Legends, Colt Express, and Wyatt Earp.

Espionage: Prepare a martini shaken, not stirred, as you play Conspiracy: The Solomon Gambit (a terrific remake of the original 1973 Conspiracy), Spyfall, Two Rooms and a Boom, Cold War: CIA vs. KGB, and Specter Ops.

Archaeology: You'll look best in a fedora as you whip through competitive games like Tikal, Tobago, Thebes (no, I'm not sure why so many archaeological games start with *T*), and Karuba, along with the cooperative Escape: The Curse of the Temple.

Pirates: Danger lurks above the ocean and beneath it in games like Forgotten Waters, Francis Drake, Treasure Island, Dead Men Tell No Tales, and Cartagena.

Other options for a themed game night include playing games by a specific designer, games published in a specific year, games that won a specific award, and games that share a core mechanic (such as social deduction games, trick-taking card games, or worker placement games).

10

Virtual Game Nights

For many people, me included, game night will always be best when it involves a group of people gathered around the same table. Still, you may someday find yourself in a position where you want to host a game night with friends and family who, for whatever reason—perhaps they're far-flung around the globe, or maybe you're all living under stay-at-home orders during a pandemic—cannot gather in the same space. There are some excellent options if you'd like to play online, and with a bit of technology and an occasional dose of creativity, game night can go on!

As you might imagine, there are some different factors to account for when you're hosting virtually, such as using the best service, making sure the technology works smoothly for everyone, and avoiding distractions.

VIDEO CHAT GAMING

As the COVID-19 pandemic forced many of us to work from home for an extended period of time, it seems that we all became too familiar with free services like Zoom and Google Meet. These services

HOW TO HOST A GAME NIGHT

are good for work, but they're terrific for organizing a virtual game night.

Both Zoom and Google Meet—which I believe are the best video chat services for virtual game nights, although there are alternatives—are relatively simple to use, with documentation online to get you started. I'll focus on gaming-specific considerations.

Hosting a virtual game night requires a distinct kind of prep. Instead of cleaning your house and preparing snacks, you need to set up your camera and microphone, ensure good lighting, and know in advance what accommodations you'll have to make to account for the fact that (probably) not everyone will have access to the game's components. You may also need to remind your guests about the event's start time a little more often than usual. It can be easy to lose track of time when you're logging on to game night instead of traveling there.

One key to a successful virtual game night is to keep your camera steady. It's hard to overstate the importance of this. I highly recommend putting your camera on a tripod and to the greatest extent possible, you should avoid moving it during the game. Believe me, everyone else on the video chat will thank you. Instead of moving the camera, move components into and out of the camera's view as necessary. You can set up a separate camera—your laptop, perhaps—if you want to show your face and reactions.

During the game, you'll also need to gently prompt other players to keep things moving. When you're all around the same table, there's usually no question about when it's your turn because the person to your right just finished their turn. On a videoconference, people often lose track. Set the turn order however you like (see the section on seating arrangements in chapter 3 for more on this), but whatever you decide, write it down so you can refer to it throughout the game.

As they do at a traditional game night, players will naturally look to the host to answer any questions they have about the game. Because it's so easy to get distracted during a remote gaming experience—your guests may have other things going on in their homes—it's even more crucial that you know the game rules inside and out. And speaking of distractions, be careful to avoid any of your own.

Although you'll manage many of the game components, whenever possible it's smart to let the players handle any physical actions they're able to, such as rolling dice. It helps the experience feel a little more like a normal game night.

GAMES THAT PLAY WELL VIRTUALLY

Not every game is suited to being played over a service like Zoom or Google Meet. Heavy strategy games, especially those with many components that need to be reviewed regularly—such as cards with a lot of text—will be especially challenging. If you're determined to do it, you can play a heavy strategy game, but lighter games tend to be more successful on video chat.

Most simple are classic parlor games like Twenty Questions, Categories, and charades. The rules are easy to explain, and they don't require any special equipment. Some paper-and-pencil games also work well, including Poker Squares and Word Squares.

In Poker Squares, one player needs a deck of cards and the others only need a piece of paper and something to write with. The player with the cards draws and announces them, one at a time, and each player writes that card (for example, 4C for "four of clubs" or QH for "queen of hearts") in one of the squares on a five-by-five grid. When all twenty-five spaces are filled, players score their rows and columns based on the poker hands they've made. (Royal flush, 50; straight flush, 30; four of a kind, 16; straight, 12; full house, 10; three of a kind, 6; flush, 5; two pairs, 3; one pair, 1.)

Word Squares, the literary cousin of Poker Squares, is played with the same five-by-five grid. Here, players take turns announcing letters (repeats are fine), with everyone writing the announced letter in one of the blocks. When all the spaces are filled, each row and column is scored. Five-letter words are worth ten points each; four-letter words, five points; and three-letter words, one point.

Many published games are also easy to play on a videoconference. A few of my favorites include Just One, Rolling America, and Wits & Wagers. In each case, only one person (the host) needs a copy of the game. The following tips, although specific to these recommendations, help illustrate what's possible at a virtual game night.

To play the cooperative party game Just One on a video call, the guesser closes their eyes while the host shows the secret word to everyone else. Those players then write their clues on whatever they have handy (scratch paper is fine) and show them to one another to eliminate any duplicates. At that point, the guesser opens their eyes to study the remaining clues and guess the secret word.

Rolling America, a roll-and-write game in which players fill in a map of the United States, requires each player to have a copy of the scoresheet—easily accomplished by having the player who owns the game send a photograph of the scoresheet to the other players, who can then print it out. For a different challenge, a BoardGameGeek user has posted a variant called Rolling Sherlock, in which the map is a profile of the detective.

For Wits & Wagers, only the host needs to own a copy. The other players need something to write on. Each time the host reads a question, players write their answers and—once everyone's finished—show the answers to the host, who writes them on the dry-erase boards included with the game and positions them on the main game board. For the bidding round, it's probably simplest for players to reveal their bids simultaneously. Two industrious Wits & Wagers fans have created excellent tools that some will prefer for remote play. A Google Slides (compatible with PowerPoint) version is available by finding the "Wits and Wagers Board for Remote Play (Google Slides)" thread on BoardGameGeek, and a Google Sheets (compatible with Excel) version is available in the "Remote-Friendly Wits & Wagers (Google Sheets)" thread.

Other party games and light strategy games that are likewise remote-friendly include Boggle, Can't Stop, Codenames, Liar's Dice, Spyfall, Wavelength, and Welcome To . . . The list expands dramatically if everyone playing owns a copy of the game.

Heavier strategy games that work well on video chat tend to share a few traits, most notably relatively simple components with no small or hard-to-read text or iconography. Many players have had success with Detective, Disney Villainous, and Forgotten Waters. Rodney Smith of Watch It Played produced a great YouTube video showing how to play Disney Villainous remotely, and Portal Games has done the same for Detective. Many of the tips in those videos can be applied to any game. Plaid Hat Games went a step further and added an entire remote-play component to its app for Forgotten Waters. In some cases, though, if you're looking to play a deep strategy game remotely, you're better off using an online gaming service.

Roleplaying games are also terrific on video chat. Dungeons & Dragons, first published in 1974, celebrated what publisher Wizards of the Coast called the "biggest year in franchise history" in 2019. Other great options include Fiasco, which thrusts players into a twisted plot reminiscent of a Coen Brothers movie; Blades in the Dark, where players are scoundrels seeking riches in an industrial fantasy city; and Lady Blackbird, a free game set in a world of adventure and romance.

A new option likely to appeal to those who host regular virtual game nights and don't want to be limited in their game selection is Vorpal Board, a system that allows you to play any tabletop game over the internet. The components seem simple: a card-scanning box, an arm to mount your phone over the board, and a hosting service that ties everything together. But the software at the heart of Vorpal Board is both sophisticated and user-friendly, making it a joy to play games remotely. Check the Vorpal Board YouTube channel for examples of how the system works.

ONLINE GAMING SERVICES

Many popular board games are available to play online from services that are more traditionally home to video games, such as Xbox Live and the PlayStation Store. Rather than try to cover every possible way board games can be played online, I'll focus on a handful of services that are dedicated to tabletop games, including Board Game Arena, Tabletopia, Tabletop Simulator, and Yucata.

My favorite is Board Game Arena, which offers free and paid membership levels and gets overwhelmingly positive reviews for its design and intuitive controls. It boasts more than two hundred games, including favorites like Carcassonne, Sushi Go!, and 7 Wonders; more than four million users; and millions of games played each month. Board Game Arena is accessed via the Web and is compatible with most browsers. For me, the major advantages of Board Game Arena are the ease of use and the fact that rules are automatically enforced so you don't have to worry about someone accidentally making a play that's not legal and figuring out how to take it back. There's no way for the players to mess something up, unintentionally or otherwise. Some other services provide a simple virtual game table, requiring players to know the rules and keep a close eye on everyone else. That's what happens at an in-person game night, but it feels like more of a chore when you're playing online.

At Board Game Arena, games can be played either in real time or in turn-based mode, which means that players don't need to be online at the same time. (Predictably, turn-based games can take much longer than real-time games.) Tournaments are scheduled regularly for many of the most popular games. One of the advantages to signing up for a paid account (becoming a premium player) is that you can have audio and video chats within Board Game Arena. It's possible to use another service, such as FaceTime or Discord, to chat during games, but the ability to do it within Board Game Arena itself is a definite advantage. Premium players also get access to game statistics.

Other games available on Board Game Arena include classics like checkers, Reversi, and Yahtzee, along with modern games such as Can't Stop, Downforce, Hanabi, Kingdomino, Race for the Galaxy, Terra Mystica, and Through the Ages. All games can be played by any members, but some can only be started by players with paid accounts. I've played hundreds of games at Board Game Arena and the only technical issue I've ever faced is an occasionally slow server. It's my go-to site for online gaming.

Tabletopia offers more than a thousand games, all of which are officially licensed versions or in the public domain, but its virtual tabletop—also browser-based (although an app version is available)—is less developed than Board Game Arena's. Whereas Board Game Arena automatically enforces the rules of a game, with Tabletopia you get a "sandbox"—images on your screen that look like a table with the game and its components waiting for you to manipulate. From there, the players handle most things more or less manually, including placing pieces on the board, drawing cards, and calculating the score. This makes it easier to add games to the service (one reason for the larger catalog), but less user-friendly and more time-consuming. Tabletopia's user interface has a steep learning curve, although it's better than Tabletop Simulator's. Like Board Game Arena, Tabletopia offers free and paid membership levels. Games can also be purchased individually if you prefer that to the subscription model.

Tabletop Simulator, like Tabletopia, doesn't enforce the rules of games played on its service. Unlike Tabletopia, however, it doesn't run in a browser. Rather, a separate app must be purchased and downloaded from Steam or another official outlet. Tabletop Simulator offers some powerful options for players willing to dig into the service and learn how to use all of its features. Roleplayers can build entire RPG dungeons, for example, while game designers and developers can use it to playtest games remotely. Some of the licensed games available on Tabletop Simulator for an additional fee include Wingspan, Scythe, and Zombicide. However, the bulk of the games here have been uploaded by users, which means they're not officially authorized by the designer or publisher—and sometimes that leads to games being taken down. User-generated content also means that the player experience on Tabletop Simulator can be inconsistent. Like Tabletopia, Tabletop Simulator has a steep learning curve and can be frustrating at times.

Yucata.de, a German website that's available in English, provides free access to more than 150 licensed games, such as Campaign Manager 2008, Castles of Burgundy, El Grande, Machi Koro, Port Royal, and St. Petersburg. Like Board Game Arena, Yucata enforces the rules of each game. One major difference between Yucata and Board Game Arena is that Yucata only offers turn-based games, nothing in real time.

All four of these services—Board Game Arena, Tabletopia, Tabletop Simulator, and Yucata—have die-hard fans who swear by them. Finding the one that's right for you is a matter of browsing the games available at each and giving them a shot. (*The Secret Cabal Gaming Podcast* has a terrific YouTube video comparing Tabletopia to Tabletop Simulator.) Other popular services include Roll20.net, which focuses on roleplaying games, BoardSpace.net, which primarily features abstract games, and Boiteajeux.net, which features Agricola, Dixit, Tzolk'in, and other modern strategy games. Dominion Online allows players to enjoy Dominion and its many expansions, while CodenamesGame.com is a great way to set up online games of Codenames.

Conclusion:
Thanks for the (Gaming) Memories

One of my favorite memories is traveling with my wife to McKinney, Texas, in April 2013 to visit my parents. During our stay, we played three card games: Wizard, Circus Flohcati, and Crazy Derby. Two years later, my father died. My mother went to be with him a few months after that. Our trip to McKinney wasn't the last time I saw them, but there was something pure and wonderful about Beth and me sitting around my parents' kitchen table and playing those games with Mom and Dad. I can't articulate exactly what it is about that specific game night, but remembering it fills me with peace and joy.

Before things get too sentimental, I can point to at least one other time we played a game with my parents and I proceeded to completely block it from my memory. Recently, while selecting some games to donate to a local thrift store, Beth and I opened our copy of Therapy: The Game, a party game published in 1986. Inside, we found a completed scoresheet with the names Erik, Beth, Jim, and Jeanne at the top. Which means we played Therapy: The Game with my parents. Which is terrifying, because some of the questions in the game are along these lines: "Who's more likely to be aroused reading a pornographic novel: A sixteen-year-old boy, or a sixteen-year-old girl?"

Setting aside the obvious mental repression related to Therapy: The Game, so many of my favorite memories are centered around board games and card games. I'm forever grateful to the designers who spend months and years of their lives creating such wonderful ways for us to spend time with one another and the publishers who take the risk of printing those games and making them available.

Millions of people around the world have similar treasured memories tied to board games and game nights. After all, that's why we play these games. It's not about winning or losing. We play for the fun, and we gather . . .

To create memories with family:

Dave Bernazzani looks back fondly on Friday nights in the early 1980s when he played Trivial Pursuit—not without some disagreement—with his family. "We would get pizza or subs from this local shop," he says. "Then we would break out the game and play until my older brother and father would get into an argument over the accuracy of an answer printed on the card and they would storm away from the table, leaving me to thumb through the cards on my own. I'd love to have some of those awesome times back again." As would I—my father was a master at Trivial Pursuit. We often played the game so that it was Dad versus everyone. Dad always won.

Andy DiNunzio recalls a childhood stay in the hospital. "My grandmother would come to visit and bring Stratego," he says. "I also learned to enjoy playing backgammon with her. Many great memories." Mark Jackson also remembers playing games with his grandmother. "I would sit on the floor with my grandma playing Monopoly, and my dad talked about how she did the same thing with him and his friends when he was young."

Greg Clensy recalls one particular game of Dixit with a dozen family members. "They weren't particularly close, not even particularly friendly," he says. "They had never played Dixit before, and we played in teams of two. The interactions of teammates and opposing teams were so funny as everyone's personalities and friendships came out. Lots of funny moments and inside jokes that are still used today."

To create memories with friends:

In the 1979 film *The Muppet Movie*, Gonzo sings about "old friends who've just met." Game nights have a way of helping people find that kind of relationship. Bayard Catron met many of his best friends at a game night on Halloween in 2007. The group hit it off immediately and they still get together regularly today.

For Leo Tischer, games provided a way to help in times of grief. He remembers "game nights after my father passed away and after my mother passed away. It was very uplifting to get together with friends and get immersed in a game. It got me smiling again."

Tami Whitsett also found comfort in gaming in the midst of tragedy. "My best friend had just been murdered," she says. "Then my cat died, I'd had two surgeries back-to-back, and I was broke." She wasn't able to afford the admission fee for a local game convention that was taking place, but she did visit to say hello and drop off some games she wanted to sell. "I stopped in to tell the organizer what was going on and burst into tears because I was so broken," Tami says. "Everyone surrounded me with hugs and love. I don't know what happened, if someone paid for my convention pass or if it was comped, but suddenly I was told that I was to stay and play games and to come back for the rest of the convention. It makes my heart warm to know that there was so much love cultivated over board and card games."

To build community:

Playing board games together often leads people to make connections that would have been impossible otherwise. Scott Tepper attended a gaming Meetup in Chicago with a friend and wound up stuck at a table playing a game he didn't particularly like. At another table, he saw the game Domaine, one of his favorites. Before he left, Scott gave his email address to the man who had brought Domaine and invited him to his next game day. The man, Tim, reached out and asked if he could bring his fiancée, Lindsay, who wasn't much of a gamer. Scott said yes, of course, and told him the next game day was set for New Year's Eve. At one point, Scott, Tim, and Lindsay wound up at a table with five of Scott's friends playing The Poll Game, a party game where players answer yes or no to questions and guess how many other players will say yes. The questions tend to be innocuous, along the lines of "Do you have a valid passport?"

"We were playing for a little while and learned that Tim and Lindsay had recently moved to Chicago, didn't know very many people, and that Lindsay was in seminary school to become a minister," Scott says. "I should mention that I and my five friends at the table are all gay and had known each other for years. One of them, Brian, is an admitted troublemaker." At one point, Brian decided the questions on the card were "too tame" so he made up his own: "Have you ever been in a three-way?" Scott was embarrassed that this was how Tim and Lindsay were being introduced to the group and asked Brian to pick a different question. But Brian insisted. "So everyone secretly made their votes," Scott says. When the answers were revealed, Tim and Lindsay both said no—but everyone else at the table said yes. Tim and Lindsay guessed there would be zero or one yes answers.

"I was mortified," Scott says. "But they were nonplussed and ended up staying at the party until 1 a.m." The two went on to become regulars in Scott's game group, and when they were married several years later, Scott was Lindsay's bridesman. Years after that, he did a reading at the ceremony where she became a minister.

Sometimes, deep friendships lead to creative approaches to problems. At Joe Cook's weekly poker game, he and his friends found an effective way to end silly arguments. "One night, someone brought old boxing gloves and headgear to 'settle all disputes,' " Joe says. "They were only used once or twice, but their very presence ended all of the drama."

Greg J. Schloesser says "perhaps my favorite gaming experience is playing Pandemic Legacy: Season 1. We played over the course of six Saturdays and had an incredible time with the game and enjoying each other's company." (As I mentioned in chapter 2, I played Pandemic Legacy: Season 1 with a group of friends over a single weekend, Friday through Sunday. It was intense and great and we'll be talking about it for years to come.)

To create unforgettable moments:

Sometimes a brilliant move or a wildly unlikely outcome cements a gaming memory. Michelle Zentis taught the original Pandemic to three new players at a Games Club of Maryland event soon after the game was released. "At various points we were completely out of one of the disease cube colors, so one person did nothing but run around removing those cubes for a few turns," she says. (If you run out of a color and need to put one more cube of that color on the board, you lose.) "We ended up winning the game on the very last possible turn, with one card in the draw deck and seven outbreaks."

Dominic Crapuchettes, designer of Evolution and Wits & Wagers, remembers playing A Game of Thrones, the board game based on George R. R. Martin's fantasy novels. "I played a super-risky move to counter a backstabbing attack and got away with it," he says. (Sounds exactly like something that would happen in the novels or the television show based on them.) "I had no right winning the battle. He just flubbed it because he didn't think I'd have the nerve to play so poorly."

Jeremy Thigpen taught his son and four of his friends Shadows over Camelot on his son's fourteenth birthday. "There was a traitor in their midst," he says. The group roleplayed and methodically used logic to identify the turncoat, a process Jeremy says "made my night. My son still talks about that game and his friends want to come over and play it again and again."

To tie generations together:

My friend Eileen Flinn grew up in the Brighton Heights neighborhood of Pittsburgh. Her family had a weekly game night, usually after dinner on Saturdays. They took turns picking the game, and Eileen, her mother, and her sisters would choose a variety of games. But her father never varied. When Kurt Flinn was in charge, the game was always Parcheesi. "I'm pretty sure we all knew how to play Parcheesi before we could ride a bike," Eileen says. "I asked my grandma about it once and she said it was one of the first birthday gifts my dad received as a child when he, my grandma, and Aunt Kate came to the United States from Austria after World War II. My grandpa, who adopted my dad and my aunt after he married my grandma, apparently taught my dad how to play and it was one of their favorite things to do."

The game nights did not end when Eileen and her sisters moved out and Kurt retired from boilermaking. Many times, Kurt and his wife, Kathleen (Eileen's mom), played Parcheesi with Kathleen's brother, Danny, and his wife, Terry. Eventually, Kathleen told Kurt that the games—which often continued the next morning—needed to move from the dining room table to the small breakfast room off the kitchen. ("We never used it for breakfast," Eileen recalls, "because it was drafty and cold.") Kurt saw the move as an opportunity to build the Parcheesi table of his dreams. It took a full weekend to design and build a table for four (the maximum number that can play Parcheesi) that fit perfectly into the eight-foot-by-eight-foot room. Made of pine and topped with tinted Lexan, a durable polycarbonate, the table is optimized for the game board: there are precisely four inches from the edge of the board to the edge of the table on every side.

"It was, and still is, a beautiful table," Eileen says. And once Kurt finished building it, "he decided a regular old Parcheesi board wasn't fit for it. He then proceeded to make his own Parcheesi board out of Lexan. He also made four sets of 'men' in red, yellow, green, and blue for him, my mom, my uncle, and my aunt, and they each had their own dice. To carry their men and dice, they each used an Altoids tin."

When her father passed away in March 2019, Eileen and her family placed the Altoids tin containing his pieces ("he always played the blue men") and dice inside his casket. They had done something similar when her uncle Danny passed away in 2017. "I like to think of the two of them holding family Parcheesi tournaments with other loved ones," Eileen says.

Whether your favorite gaming memories involve Connect 4 and Hungry Hungry Hippos, Ticket to Ride and Pandemic, or Gloomhaven and Brass: Birmingham, I hope this book will help you make more great memories in the future. Games have played an important role in my life, and many of my closest friends started as strangers on the other side of the table. We've grown together and shared triumphs and tragedies, both on the game board and in our personal lives. We've laughed and cried and laughed so hard we cried. And we always look forward to gathering again.

I'd love to hear all about your favorite game nights. Find me on Twitter @ErikBoardGames and on my Facebook page, About Board Games.

Game on!

Acknowledgments

My deep thanks to the many people who helped this book come to life:

My wife, Elizabeth—my first love, first reader, first editor, and first choice to play games with.

My superb editor at Tiller Press, Hannah Robinson, and the entire Tiller Press team.

All of my colleagues at The Opinionated Gamers, including those who contributed reviews for this book: our fearless leader Dale Yu, Matt Carlson, Eric Eden, Alan How, Jeff Lingwall, Tery Noseworthy, Melissa Rogerson, Chris Wray, and last but not least, game guru extraordinaire Mark Jackson.

The game designers whose creations make this such a wonderful hobby, including Alan R. Moon, Rob Daviau, Matt Leacock, Susan McKinley Ross, Eric Lang, Kevin Wilson, and Daryl Andrews.

Everyone who talked to me, in person and online, about how games have impacted your lives. You were incredibly generous with your time, and I appreciate all of you. Every conversation shaped this book.

Notes

INTRODUCTION

1   "Playing Board Games, Cognitive Decline and Dementia: A French Population-Based Cohort Study," National Library of Medicine, accessed June 8, 2020, https://www.ncbi.nlm.nih.gov/pmc/articles/PMC3758967/.

2   "Playing Analog Games Is Associated With Reduced Declines in Cognitive Function: A 68-Year Longitudinal Cohort Study," *The Journals of Gerontology: Series B*, accessed July 4, 2020, https://academic.oup.com/psych socgerontology/article/75/3/474/5628188.

3   "Baduk (the Game of Go) Improved Cognitive Function and Brain Activity in Children with Attention Deficit Hyperactivity Disorder," *Psychiatry Investigation*, accessed June 8, 2020.

4   "Kickstarter and Games in 2019," ICO Partners, accessed June 8, 2020, https://icopartners.com/2020/01/kickstarter-and-games-in-2019/.

5   "Frosthaven by Isaac Childres," Kickstarter, accessed June 8, 2020, https://www.kickstarter.com/projects/frosthaven/frosthaven.

6   "Hasbro Reports Revenue and Operating Profit Growth for the Full-Year and Fourth Quarter 2019," *Business Wire*, accessed June 8, 2020, https://www.businesswire.com/news/home/20200211005498/en/Hasbro-Reports-Revenue-Operating-Profit-Growth-Full-Year.

7   "Hasbro Reports Revenue, Operating Profit and Net Earnings Growth for Full-Year 2015," Hasbro, accessed June 8, 2020, https://hasbro.gcs-web.com/news-releases/news-release-details/hasbro-reports-revenue-operating-profit-and-net-earnings-0.

CHAPTER 2

1   "Couples Creating Art or Playing Board Games Release 'Love Hormone' — but Men who Paint Release Most," Baylor University, accessed June 8, 2020, https://www.baylor.edu/mediacommunications/news.php?action=story&story=206875.

2   "Oxytocin and Social Bonds: The Role of Oxytocin in Perceptions of Romantic Partners' Bonding Behavior," National Library of Medicine, accessed June 8, 2020, https://pubmed.ncbi.nlm.nih.gov/28968183/.

CHAPTER 4

1   Dr. Melissa Rogerson, Martin Gibbs, and Wally Smith, "More than the sum of their bits: Understanding the gameboard and components," in *Rerolling*

Boardgames: Essays on Themes, Systems, Experiences and Ideologies, eds. Douglas Brown and Esther MacCallum-Stewart (Jefferson, NC: McFarland & Company, 2020).

2   "Weight as an Embodiment of Importance," National Library of Medicine, accessed June 8, 2020, https://pubmed.ncbi.nlm.nih.gov/19686292/.

3   Rogerson, Gibbs, and Smith, "More than the sum of their bits."

Game Index

Werewolf, 66, 78, 92
  Artifacts expansion, 93
  One Night Ultimate Werewolf, 73–74, 87, 143
  Ultimate Werewolf: Deluxe Edition, 92–93
Western Legends, 144
Where's the Money, Lebowski?, 16
Whistle Stop, 144
Wingspan, xv, 49–50, 85, 136–37, 154
Winner's Circle, 141
Winter Wonderland, 94
Witness, 136

Wits & Wagers, xiv-xv, 50, 150–51, 159
Wizard, 155
Word Squares, 149, 150
World Cup Tournament Football, 140
Wyatt Earp, 144

Xia: Legends of a Drift System, 10

Yahtzee, 153

Zombicide, 45, 78, 142–43, 154
Zombie Dice, 109–10

About the Author

Erik Arneson is a lifelong tabletop game enthusiast and former newspaper reporter who has written hundreds of articles about games for such publications as *The Spruce*, *Knucklebones*, *Counter*, and on The Opinionated Gamers website. The author of *17 Games You Can Play Right Now!*, he has been a featured speaker on the topic of board game publicity at the American International Toy Fair and is regularly cited as a board game expert. He and his wife, Elizabeth, are both part owners of the greatest franchise in all of professional sports—the Green Bay Packers—and live near Harrisburg, Pennsylvania.